Home Cooking

WITH AMY COLEMAN

Volume 2

Based on the Public Television Series
SPONSORED BY KITCHENAID

WITH **AMY COLEMAN**

Volume 2

Produced by Marjorie Poore Productions

Photography by Darla Furlani

M PP

Contents

Introduction

I grew up in a time when mothers, more *often than not, were always home to greet their children after school. In our home, it was a family priority to have our dinner meal together, usually served at 6:00 p.m., no matter how many football, wrestling, or swimming practices were being juggled.*

Some of my fondest childhood memories *are the welcoming smells that came from the kitchen as my mom and my grandmother cooked. They used few, if any, convenience products. No boxed, canned, styrofoam-trayed, microwavable, or boiled-in-a-bag type of food. Just the real stuff. Milk from Carl and Creedie's farm cows next door—unpasteurized and unhomogenized. The eggs were from Mr. and Mrs. Miller, our other neighbors. The fruits and vegetables came from our own garden and were canned or frozen to last throughout the year. It was economical, wholesome, and healthy. It was satisfying. It was real!*

Nutritional, low-fat, no-fat, low-calorie, *and low-sodium foods were not feverishly pursued as they often seem to be today. Our food was inherently good for us because it was fresh, unprocessed, well-balanced, and eaten in moderation. We understood where the ingredients came from, how they were grown and harvested, what they were like in their natural, state.*

Besides satisfying our physical needs, *our family meals gave us unity. During dinner and around the kitchen table, we learned table manners. We learned the art of conversation and found out what happened in each other's days. We learned to appreciate each other's personalities and characteristics. It was a time for us to engage, not disengage with other distractions like television.*

It was only natural that I carried these *home cooking traditions into my adult life, where they have become part of my heritage and culture. My family's home cooking today is based largely on my mother's cooking and her mother's cooking. We continue to share a family recipe collection that thrives, renews itself, and brings so much pleasure to so many people.*

In many ways, the *Home Cooking* television series is another extension of these traditions. Each program includes a guest cookbook author invited to share their favorite recipes from their cookbooks. We cook, have fun, share tips, secrets, mistakes, successes, and enjoy the process of creating wonderful food together. Our authors bring to the show a wealth of different kinds of foods from different cuisines. Our goal? To inspire and encourage people to get into the kitchen—not out of obligation or routine— but for the enjoyment and pleasure of preparing delicious recipes for themselves, their friends, and their families.

In this book, you will find all the wonderful recipes we made on the programs in the second part of the series. Having tasted all of them, I can report that every single one of them is delicious and easy to prepare. I am pleased to share them with you and hope that you, your family, friends, and loved ones will enjoy them as much as we have.

—Amy Coleman

✱ Acknowledgments

The recipes in this book are from the second season of HOME COOKING *with Amy Coleman, which airs on PBS stations across the country. From the beginning, the series has been generously supported by* **KitchenAid Portable Appliances**, *the exclusive sponsor of the television programs. KitchenAid's backing of this series is further proof of their unending commitment to provide home cooks with not only the highest quality kitchen tools, but also the recipes and skills to make wonderful, home-cooked meals. Special thanks to Brian Maynard for his positive energy, enthusiasm, and great ideas. Thanks also to Tom Welke and the many others at KitchenAid who have continued to provide invaluable support to the project.*

We'd also like to thank all the cookbook authors and culinary professionals who traveled to Vancouver to appear on the programs: Mary Corpening Barber, Rick Bayless, Denis Blais, Georgeanne Brennan, Lora Brody, Shirley Corriher, Claire Criscuolo, Narsai David, Marcel Desaulniers, Diane Kochilas, Soren Fakstorp, Janet Fletcher, Rozanne Gold, Chris Johnson, Zella Junkin, Barbara Kafka, Tom Lacalamita, Nick Malgieri, James McNair, Mai Pham, Tori Ritchie, Michel Roux, Sara Corpening, Chris Schlesinger, Stephen Wong, and T. K. Woods.

A special thank you to the following companies, who generously donated props for the TV programs and the cookbook: Benziger Family Winery, Caleco, Carr's Crackers, Casafina, Catskill's cutting boards, Colavita Italian Food Products, Fiori Ware, Illy Espresso, Mango Imports, Signature Housewares, and Waechtersbach.

Finally, we owe a big thanks to the wonderful and talented staff at the Canadian Broadcasting Corporation in Vancouver, where we taped the shows, and the loyal and devoted members of our production team who made so many fine contributions to the series: Raazhan Rae, Eric Belanger, and Becca Burrington. Also, a big thank you to Kari Perin, Kristen Wurz, and Cate Conniff Dobrich for the excellent work and diligent efforts in putting this book together.

—Marjorie Poore and Alec Fatalevich

BREADS & BREAKFAST

Sizzling Saigon Crêpes

MAI PHAM / REPRINTED FROM *THE BEST OF THAI AND VIETNAMESE COOKING* (PRIMA PUBLISHING)

Batter

2 cups rice flour
1/4 cup all-purpose flour
1 cup unsweetened coconut milk
2 cups water
3 green onions, thinly sliced
1/2 teaspoon salt
1 teaspoon sugar
2 teaspoons curry powder
1 teaspoon ground turmeric

Filling

4 tablespoons vegetable oil
1 yellow onion, very thinly sliced
1/2 pound boneless, skinless chicken breast, thinly sliced and then cubed
12 medium-size raw shrimp, peeled, deveined, and halved lengthwise
4 cups bean sprouts
2 cups white mushrooms, thinly sliced

1 cup Vietnamese Dipping Sauce (*see below*)
Lettuce and mint leaves

SERVES 4

FOR smaller CRÊPES, USE A SMALLER PAN. REMEMBER TO USE less batter, AS A THICK CRÊPE WILL BE CHEWY.

✱ In a large mixing bowl, whisk together all of the batter ingredients. Set aside.

✱ In a 10-inch frying or omelet pan, heat 1 tablespoon of the oil over high heat. Add about 1 tablespoon of the onion, 2 tablespoons of the chicken, and 6 of the shrimp halves and toss in pan until the shrimp turns opaque, about 20 seconds. Whisk the batter well, then ladle about 2/3 cup of the batter into the pan, tilting it so that the batter completely covers the surface of the pan. Reduce heat to moderate. Pile 1 cup of bean sprouts and 1/2 cup of mushrooms on one side of the crêpe, closer to the center than the edge. Reduce heat to low. Cover with a lid and cook for another 3 minutes, making sure the bottom doesn't burn.

✱ Remove lid from pan and let crêpe cook for another 2 minutes to dry out the batter. To remove the crêpe, lift the side without the bean sprouts and fold over. Using a spatula, gently slide the crêpe onto a large plate.

✱ Wipe the pan clean and cook the other 3 crêpes. Serve crêpes with Vietnamese Dipping Sauce. Tear off a bite-size piece of the crêpe, wrap with lettuce and mint, and dip in sauce.

Vietnamese Dipping Sauce

2 small garlic cloves, sliced thinly
1 teaspoon ground chili paste
1 fresh Thai bird chili, chopped (optional)
1/4 cup fish sauce

2/3 cup hot water
2 tablespoons fresh lime juice with pulp
1/4 cup sugar
2 tablespoons shredded carrots for garnish

✱ Place garlic, chili paste, and chili in a mortar. With a pestle, pound into a paste. If you do not have a mortar and pestle, finely mince the garlic and chili and combine with chili paste.

✱ Combine the garlic mixture with the remaining ingredients in a small mixing bowl. Stir until the sugar is dissolved. Ladle the sauce into serving bowls and float the carrots on top.

Australian Flax and Sesame Bread

NARSAI DAVID, FOOD AND WINE EDITOR, KCBS RADIO, SAN FRANCISCO, CALIFORNIA

1/3 cup whole wheat berries
2 1/2 cups water
1 tablespoon active dry yeast
1 cup whole wheat flour
4 cups bread flour or all-purpose flour

2 tablespoons vegetable oil
2 tablespoons malt powder
1 1/2 teaspoons salt
1/3 cup flax seed, toasted
1/2 cup sesame seeds

✳ In a small saucepan, steam the wheat berries slowly with 1/2 cup of the water until the water is absorbed. Set aside to cool.

✳ Mix all ingredients except sesame seeds in a large mixing bowl and stir well. The dough can be kneaded either by hand or a stand mixer with a dough hook.

✳ To make the bread by hand, turn dough out onto a floured surface and knead it until it is smooth and elastic, approximately 10 minutes. If using a stand mixer, knead the dough at low speed for 8 to 10 minutes.

✳ Place dough in a clean, large bowl. Cover with a kitchen towel. Set it in a warm, dry place to rise until dough has just about doubled in bulk, about 60 to 75 minutes.

✳ When the dough has doubled, turn it out onto a floured surface, punch it down, and divide into 2 pieces. Form round loaves, taking time to round them up evenly until there are no wrinkles on top of the loaves. Moisten the loaves with a wet towel or a sprayer and roll in a bowl of sesame seeds.

✳ Place the loaves on a sheet pan dusted with flour or cornmeal (or onto a peel directly if you plan to bake on a baking stone). Cover loaves with a towel on the counter and let them rise until almost doubled, about one hour.

✳ With a razor blade, cut 4 deep gashes to form a very large square on the surface of each loaf. Cover again with the towel, and let the dough rise another 10 to 15 minutes.

✳ While the loaves are rising, preheat the oven to 400°F with a rack positioned so that the bread will bake in the middle of the oven. If using a baking stone, it should be heating in the oven at the same time. Place the loaves in the oven and spray them well with a fine mist of water. Repeat the misting 2 more times at 10-minute intervals. Bake for about 45 minutes until a nice firm crust has formed. Test the doneness by rapping the bottom with your knuckle. The loaf should be firm and make a hollow sound. Cool on a wire rack.

MAKES 2 LOAVES

BREAD MAKING IS easy WHEN USING A STAND MIXER, WHICH DOES ALL OF THE WORK FOR YOU. THIS wonderful RECIPE IS FROM NARSAI DAVID, SAN FRANCISCO'S WIDELY loved FOOD PERSONALITY.

Touch of Grace Biscuits

SHIRLEY CORRIHER / REPRINTED FROM *COOKWISE* **(WILLIAM MORROW AND COMPANY)**

MAKES 10 BISCUITS

THE secret OF THESE

FEATHERY BISCUITS IS A

dough SO WET THAT

IT MUST BE FLOURED IN

ORDER TO BE HANDLED.

THE LIQUID IN A WET

DOUGH SUCH AS THIS

TURNS TO steam IN

A HOT OVEN, CREATING

A POWERFUL LEAVENER.

Nonstick cooking spray
1 1/2 cups Southern self-rising flour (*see note*)
1/8 teaspoon baking soda
1/3 teaspoon salt
1 tablespoon sugar
3 tablespoons shortening

1 to 1 1/4 cups buttermilk or 3/4 cup
   buttermilk and 1/2 cup heavy cream
1 cup bleached all-purpose flour for
   shaping dough
2 tablespoons butter, melted

✽ Preheat the oven to 475°F and spray an 8-inch round cake pan with nonstick cooking spray.

✽ In a medium mixing bowl, combine the flour, soda, salt, and sugar. With your fingers or a pastry cutter, work the shortening into the flour mixture until there are no shortening lumps larger than a big pea.

✽ Stir in the buttermilk and let stand for 2 to 3 minutes. This dough is so wet you cannot shape it in the usual manner.

✽ Pour the cup of all-purpose flour onto a plate or pie tin. Flour your hands well. Spoon a biscuit-size lump of wet dough into the flour and sprinkle some flour over the wet dough to coat the outside. Pick up the biscuit and shape it roughly into a soft round. At the same time shake off any excess flour. The dough is so soft that it will not hold its shape. As you shape each biscuit, place it in the pan. Push the biscuits tightly against each other so that they will rise up and not spread out. Continue shaping biscuits in this manner until all the dough is used. (To make a large batch of biscuits in a hurry, spray a medium-size—about 2-inch—ice cream scoop with nonstick cooking spray. Cover a jelly roll pan with all-purpose flour. Quickly scoop biscuits onto the flour, sprinkle with flour, shape, and place in small pans.)

✽ Brush the biscuits with melted butter and bake just above the center of the oven until lightly browned, about 15 to 20 minutes. Cool for 1 or 2 minutes in the pan, then dump out and cut the biscuits apart. Split biscuits in half, butter, and eat immediately.

NOTE: If low-protein Southern self-rising flour is not available, use 1 cup all-purpose and 1/2 cup instant (such as Wondra or Shake and Blend) or cake flour, plus 1/2 teaspoon baking powder. If self-rising flour is not available, use a total of 1 1/2 teaspoons baking powder. Do not use self-rising flour for the shaping, since the leavener will give a bitter taste to the outside of the biscuits.

Summer Squash Frittata

TORI RITCHIE / REPRINTED FROM *CABIN COOKING* (TIME-LIFE BOOKS)

2 tablespoons olive oil, plus oil as needed
2 yellow crookneck squash, diced
3 pattypan squash, diced
2 tablespoons chopped fresh oregano or
   1 tablespoon dried oregano

Salt and freshly ground black pepper
6 eggs
2 tablespoons warm water
3 ounces Italian fontina cheese, cut into
   small pieces

✱ In a heatproof 8-inch frying pan placed over medium-high heat, warm the 2 tablespoons of olive oil. Add the diced squash and cook, stirring occasionally, until softened and lightly browned, about 8 minutes. Stir in the oregano and season to taste with salt and pepper.

✱ Preheat a broiler. Meanwhile, in a small bowl, lightly beat the eggs with the water, then stir in the cheese. When the squash is ready, spread it in an even layer in the frying pan; if the pan seems dry, pour in a little more olive oil to coat it. Pour in the egg-cheese mixture. When it begins to set, lift the edge with a wooden spoon to let the uncooked eggs flow underneath. Continue to cook until the top of the frittata looks fairly dry, about 4 minutes.

✱ Transfer the pan to the broiler, placing it about 6 inches below the heat source. Broil until the top of the frittata looks puffed and golden, about 3 minutes. Remove from the broiler, cut into wedges, and serve directly from the pan.

SERVES 4

A frittata IS A FLAT, ITALIAN-STYLE OMELET IN WHICH THE filling IS mixed WITH THE EGGS. IF ITALIAN FONTINA IS NOT AVAILABLE, SUBSTITUTE MONTEREY JACK CHEESE.

Neapolitan Ricotta, Mozzarella, and Prosciutto Pie

NICK MALGIERI / REPRINTED FROM *HOW TO BAKE* (HARPERCOLLINS)

Dough
3 cups unbleached all-purpose flour
1/2 cup sugar
1 teaspoon salt
1 teaspoon baking powder
12 tablespoons (1 1/2 sticks) cold unsalted
    butter
3 large eggs

Filling
2 pounds whole-milk or part-skim ricotta
6 large eggs
1 teaspoon freshly ground black pepper
1/4 cup grated Pecorino Romano cheese
1 pound mozzarella, coarsely grated
1/2 pound sweet dried sausage, peeled
    and diced
1/2 pound prosciutto, shredded
1/2 cup chopped fresh flat-leaf parsley

Egg wash: 1 egg well beaten with a pinch
    of salt

SERVES 8 TO 10

THE COMBINATION OF
A sweet DOUGH AND
A SALTY FILLING YIELDS A
GOOD contrast—THE
SWEETNESS OF THE DOUGH
TEMPERS THE RATHER
salty FILLING. IF THE
COMBINATION DOES NOT
APPEAL TO YOU, LEAVE
OUT THE SUGAR; ADD A
TABLESPOON OR TWO OF
WATER TO make THE
DOUGH FORM A BALL.

✳ Butter an 11 x 17-inch jelly roll pan or a 12-inch-diameter x 2-inch-deep cake pan and set aside.

✳ To make the dough, combine the dry ingredients in the bowl of a food processor fitted with a metal blade and pulse several times to mix. Distribute the butter evenly over the dry ingredients in the work bowl. Pulse until very finely powdered. Add the eggs and continue to pulse until the dough forms into a ball on the blade.

✳ Remove the dough and divide into 2 pieces, one of which is two-thirds of the dough and the other one-third. Press the large piece into a circle and wrap in plastic. Press the smaller piece into a square and wrap in plastic, also. Refrigerate both pieces of dough while preparing the filling.

✳ To make the filling, place the ricotta in the work bowl of the food processor and pulse to purée until smooth. Transfer the ricotta to a mixing bowl and stir in the eggs, one at a time; stir in the remaining filling ingredients in the order listed.

✳ Set a rack at the lower third of the oven and preheat to 350°F.

✳ Lightly flour a work surface and the larger piece of dough and roll the dough into a 17-inch circle. Fold the dough into quarters and place in the prepared pan. Unfold the dough and press into the pan, allowing any excess dough to hang over the sides. Pour in the filling (it will come to about 1/4 inch below the top of the pan) and smooth the top.

(continued on next page)

✳ Roll the remaining dough into a 10-inch square and cut into 1-inch strips. Paint the dough strips with the egg wash. Arrange 5 strips over the filling, leaving an even amount of space between strips. Arrange the remaining strips at a 45-degree angle across the first ones, creating a basketweave effect. Press the ends of the strips against the rim of the pan to make them stick and trim away excess dough—only from the strips—around the top of the pan. Use a small knife to loosen the bottom crust dough around the rim of the pan and fold it over to create an edge for the top crust.

✳ Bake the pie for about 45 minutes, until the filling is set and the dough is baked through. Don't overbake, or the filling will become watery and soak through the bottom crust. Remove from oven and cool in the pan on a rack.

✳ To unmold, place a platter over the pie and invert it, then remove the pan. Replace the pan with another platter and invert the pizza again. Remove the top platter.

✳ Keep the pie at room temperature the day it is baked. For longer storage, wrap in plastic wrap and refrigerate for up to several days. Bring back to room temperature before serving in small wedges.

New Orleans Bread Pudding with Southern Whiskey Sauce

REPRINTED FROM *JOY OF COOKING* (SCRIBNER)

3 tablespoons unsalted butter, softened
1¼ pounds French or Italian bread
   (1½ to 2 loaves)
1 cup raisins
3 large eggs
4 cups whole milk

2 cups sugar
2 tablespoons vanilla
1 teaspoon ground cinnamon

Southern Whiskey Sauce (*see below*)

✻ Spread the butter on a 13 x 9-inch baking pan, preferably glass. Cut the bread into ½-inch slices. Arrange the slices almost upright in tightly spaced rows in the prepared pan. Tuck the raisins between the slices.

✻ Whisk the eggs in a large mixing bowl until frothy. Whisk in the milk, sugar, vanilla, and cinnamon. Pour mixture over the bread slices and let stand for 1 hour, pressing down now and then with a spatula to wet the tops of the slices.

✻ Preheat the oven to 375°F. Bake the pudding until the top is puffed and lightly browned, about 1 hour. Cover with Southern Whiskey Sauce and let stand on a rack for 30 to 60 minutes, then cut into squares and serve. Leftover sauced pudding will keep for several days in the refrigerator and can be reheated in a 300°F oven for 15 minutes.

Southern Whiskey Sauce

½ cup unsalted butter
1 cup sugar
¼ cup bourbon or other whiskey
2 tablespoons water

¼ teaspoon freshly grated or ground
   nutmeg
⅛ teaspoon salt
1 large egg

✻ In a small, heavy saucepan melt the butter over low heat. With a wooden spoon or heatproof rubber spatula, stir in the sugar, bourbon, water, nutmeg, and salt. Cook, stirring, until the sugar is dissolved and the mixture is blended. Remove from the heat.

✻ Whisk the egg until light and frothy. Vigorously whisk the egg into the liquor mixture. Set the sauce over medium heat and, stirring, bring to a simmer. Cook until thickened, about 1 minute. The sauce will not curdle. Serve at once, set aside at room temperature for 8 hours, or let cool, then cover and refrigerate for up to 3 days, reheating over low heat before using. *Makes 1½ cups*

SERVES 8 TO 12

THIS IS home COOKING AT ITS BEST. THE FINISHED DISH IS LIKE A warm STICKY BUN DRENCHED IN BUTTER AND BOURBON. THE SAUCE IS ALSO good WITH APPLE PUDDINGS OR ANY OTHER CAKE MADE WITH fruits OR NUTS. FOR A MILDER SAUCE, REPLACE HALF OF THE spirits WITH WATER.

Breakfast Pizza

BRENDA C. WARD AND JANE CABINESS JARREL / REPRINTED FROM *GOOD 'N' HEALTHY* **(TOMMY NELSON, A DIVISION OF NELSON-WORD PUBLISHING GROUP)**

1 package refrigerated crescent rolls
1 pound reduced-fat turkey sausage
1 cup frozen shredded hash browns
1 cup reduced-fat cheddar cheese, grated
5 eggs

¼ cup skim milk
Reduced-fat Parmesan cheese
2 scallions, trimmed and cut thinly on the diagonal

✱ Preheat oven to 375°F. Unroll the crescent rolls and press together to form a solid crust in a 12-inch pizza pan.

✱ Brown the turkey sausage in a skillet. Remove the sausage and drain on paper towels. Crumble sausage over pizza crust.

✱ Sprinkle frozen hash browns over turkey sausage and top with cheese.

✱ Using a wire whisk, beat the eggs with the skim milk. Pour mixture over pizza.

✱ Sprinkle top of pizza with the Parmesan cheese and scallions. Place in oven and bake for 35 minutes or until set.

SERVES 6

THIS IS A HEARTY BREAKFAST DISH FOR kids WHO WILL NOT ONLY HAVE A LOT OF fun PUTTING IT TOGETHER, BUT WILL enjoy ITS GREAT TASTE.

Puffed Oven Pancake with Summer Fruit

TORI RITCHIE / REPRINTED FROM *CABIN COOKING* **(TIME-LIFE BOOKS)**

¹/₃ cup all-purpose flour
2 tablespoons sugar
¹/₃ cup milk
3 eggs
¹/₄ cup unsalted butter

2 firm, ripe peaches or nectarines, peeled
    (if desired), pitted, and sliced
1¹/₂ cups raspberries or blackberries
2 tablespoons confectioners' sugar
Lemon wedges (optional)

✳ Preheat oven to 425°F. In a blender or food processor, process the flour, sugar, milk, and eggs until thoroughly blended. Set aside.

✳ Place a 10- to 12-inch ovenproof frying pan over medium-high heat and melt the butter. Add the peaches or nectarines and cook, stirring often, until the fruit is hot and slightly softened, 3 to 5 minutes, depending upon ripeness. Remove from the heat and scatter with the berries.

✳ Pour the egg mixture over the fruit in the pan and immediately put in the oven. Bake until puffed and golden, about 18 minutes.

✳ Remove from the oven and sift confectioners' sugar over the top. Cut into wedges to serve and, if desired, offer lemon wedges to squeeze over each portion.

Brown Sugar Bacon

TORI RITCHIE / REPRINTED FROM *CABIN COOKING* (TIME-LIFE BOOKS)

8 strips thick-cut bacon (about $3/4$ pound)

3 tablespoons firmly packed light brown sugar

✳ Preheat the broiler. Line the bottom of a slotted broiler pan with aluminum foil.

✳ On a sheet of waxed paper or foil, arrange the bacon strips side by side. Press the brown sugar through a sieve with the back of a spoon, letting it shower over the bacon strips and distributing it as evenly as possible. Rub a finger over each strip to smooth out the sugar.

✳ Transfer the strips to the slotted top of the broiler pan, twisting each strip several times to form a corkscrew as you lay it down. The strips can be close together, but should not touch. Broil 6 inches below the heat source until the edges are browned and crisp, 5 to 7 minutes: watch carefully as the sugar can burn. Turn the bacon strips gently with tongs (they will hold their shape) and broil on the second side until crisp, 2 to 3 minutes longer. Transfer to paper towels to drain. Serve warm.

SERVES 4

IF YOU DON'T have A SLOTTED BROILER PAN, YOU CAN fry THE BACON IN A NONSTICK FRYING PAN, SIEVING THE sugar OVER IT ABOUT HALFWAY THROUGH COOKING.

Cabin Potatoes

TORI RITCHIE / REPRINTED FROM *CABIN COOKING* (TIME-LIFE BOOKS)

4 large baking potatoes (about 3 pounds)
1 small red (Spanish) onion

Salt and freshly ground black pepper
4 tablespoons unsalted butter

✱ Peel the potatoes and shred on the large hole of a cheese grater or in a food processor fitted with a shredding disk. Place in a large bowl. Grate the onion into the potatoes. Season generously with salt and pepper and stir well to mix.

✱ Melt 2 tablespoons of the butter in a 10- to 12-inch nonstick frying pan over medium-high heat. Add the potato-onion mixture and spread into an even layer, pressing it down to make a "cake." Set a piece of aluminum foil large enough to cover the entire surface over the mixture. On top of the foil, place a heatproof plate that is just slightly smaller than the pan circumference so that it rests directly on the foil. Cook the potatoes, undisturbed, until the bottom is well browned, 12 to 15 minutes.

✱ Remove the plate and aluminum foil from the potato cake. Place plate, top side down, on top of the potatoes. Holding the plate and the pan with hot pads, invert them so the potato cake turns, browned side up, onto the plate. Return the pan to the heat and melt the remaining 2 tablespoons of butter. Slide the potato cake, browned side up, into the pan. Replace the aluminum foil and the plate and continue to cook, undisturbed, until well browned on the second side, about 10 minutes longer. Remove from the heat, remove the plate and foil, and slide the potatoes onto a serving plate. Cut into wedges to serve.

Dangerously Red Smoothie

MARY CORPENING BARBER, SARA CORPENING, AND LORI LYN NARLOCK / REPRINTED FROM
SMOOTHIES (CHRONICLE BOOKS)

1 cup low-fat strawberry yogurt
1/2 cup cranberry juice

1 1/2 cups hulled and quartered fresh
    strawberries, frozen (*see note*)
1 cup fresh raspberries, frozen (*see note*)

✳ Combine the yogurt and cranberry juice in a blender. Add the strawberries and raspberries; blend until smooth.

NOTE: **To freeze strawberries,** remove hulls, cut in quarters, place in plastic bags, and freeze until firm. **To freeze raspberries,** sort through berries and discard any that are moldy or spoiled. Freeze in plastic bags until firm.

SERVES 2

TASTING like A STRAW-BERRY MILKSHAKE TINGED WITH raspberries, THIS SLIGHTLY TART SMOOTHIE provides ONE AND A HALF TIMES THE RECOMMENDED DAILY ALLOWANCE OF VITAMIN C.

Dew It! Smoothie

MARY CORPENING BARBER, SARA CORPENING, AND LORI LYN NARLOCK / REPRINTED FROM
SMOOTHIES (CHRONICLE BOOKS)

2 1/2 cups diced fresh honeydew melon
2 tablespoons chopped fresh mint
1 tablespoon fresh lime juice

Pinch of salt
1/2 cup ginger ale or lemon-lime soda

✳ Place all the ingredients in a blender. Blend until smooth.

SERVES 2

THIS refreshing COMBINATION OF HONEY-DEW MELON AND MINT IS A REAL THIRST-QUENCHER, ideal AFTER A WORKOUT OR ON A HOT SUMMER DAY.

Banana Latte Smoothie

MARY CORPENING BARBER, SARA CORPENING, AND LORI LYN NARLOCK / REPRINTED FROM
SMOOTHIES **(CHRONICLE BOOKS)**

SERVES 2

THIS scrumptious

DRINK LOOKS AND TASTES

LIKE A real LATTE.

1 cup soy milk
3/4 cup strong-brewed coffee or espresso,
    room temperature or chilled
2 fresh bananas, frozen and sliced (*see
    note below*)

6 to 8 ice cubes
1 teaspoon unsweetened cocoa powder,
    for garnish
1/4 teaspoon ground cinnamon, for garnish

✱ Combine the soy milk and coffee in a blender. Add the bananas. Blend until smooth.
With the blender running, add ice cubes until they are incorporated and the desired consistency is reached. Pour into tall glasses and sprinkle with cocoa powder and cinnamon.

Classico Smoothie

MARY CORPENING BARBER, SARA CORPENING, AND LORI LYN NARLOCK / REPRINTED FROM
SMOOTHIES **(CHRONICLE BOOKS)**

SERVES 2

A favorite OF

SMOOTHIE AFICIONADOS,

THIS SIMPLE SMOOTHIE

IS high IN VITAMIN C

AND POTASSIUM.

1 cup orange juice
1 cup hulled and quartered fresh
    strawberries, frozen (*see note page 23*)

2 fresh bananas, frozen and sliced
    (*see note*)

✱ Pour the orange juice into a blender. Add the strawberries and bananas. Blend until
smooth.

NOTE: To freeze bananas, peel, place in plastic bag, and freeze. Freeze several bananas at
one time for quick use. Slice when ready to use.

STARTERS

Beef Empanadas

BARBARA KAFKA / REPRINTED FROM *PARTY FOOD* (WILLIAM MORROW AND COMPANY)

MAKES 48 EMPANADAS

A **wonderful** HORS D'OEUVRE. PLAN TO MAKE THE COMPONENTS **ahead** SO YOU'RE NOT SCRAMBLING WHEN YOUR GUESTS **arrive**.

Empanada Dough

$2^1/_4$ cups all-purpose flour

1 teaspoon kosher salt

6 tablespoons cold unsalted butter, cut into small pieces

2 eggs, lightly beaten

$1/_3$ cup ice water

Beef Empanada Filling

2 teaspoons olive oil

$1/_4$ cup finely chopped onion

2 medium cloves garlic, smashed, peeled, and minced

2 teaspoons finely chopped fresh jalapeño pepper

$1/_2$ pound ground beef

2 teaspoons kosher salt

$1^1/_2$ teaspoons ground cardamom

Freshly ground black pepper to taste

3 canned plum tomatoes, drained and roughly chopped

1 hard-boiled egg, finely chopped

2 tablespoons chopped fresh cilantro leaves

2 teaspoons fresh lime juice

Egg wash: 1 egg well beaten with a pinch of salt

✳ To make the dough, combine flour and salt in a large mixing bowl. Rub butter into flour mixture until it resembles coarse crumbs, or pulse in a food processor.

✳ Add the eggs and water and gently work the mixture together until it forms a ball; or pulse in a food processor until ingredients just combine into a loose ball. Remove dough from bowl or food processor and wrap in plastic wrap. Refrigerate for at least 2 hours.

✳ To make the filling, heat oil in a skillet over medium heat. Stir in the onion and garlic and cook for about 1 minute. Stir in the jalapeño and ground beef and cook, stirring, for about 5 minutes, or until meat has lost all pink color.

✳ Remove from heat and stir in remaining ingredients. Transfer to a bowl and allow mixture to cool completely before beginning to fill empanadas.

✳ Preheat oven to 350°F, placing a rack in the center of the oven. To fill empanadas, roll out dough on a lightly floured surface to about $1/_{16}$-inch thick. Cut out rounds with a 3-inch cookie cutter. Reroll scraps to use up all of the dough. Place 1 level teaspoon of filling in the center of each round. Lightly brush some egg wash halfway around the edge. Fold the pastry in half to form a turnover and pinch edges together to seal securely.

✳ Place empanadas on a baking sheet (not air-cushioned), lined with parchment paper. Brush tops of empanadas with egg wash and bake until golden brown, about 12 minutes. Remove from oven and allow to cool slightly before serving.

Rustic Ranch-Style Soup with Tomato, Jalapeño, and Avocado

RICK BAYLESS / REPRINTED FROM *RICK BAYLESS'S MEXICAN KITCHEN* **(SCRIBNER)**

SERVES 6 TO 8

IT IS BEST TO MAKE THIS

SOUP WITH REALLY ripe,

VINE-RIPENED TOMATOES.

ONCE THE CONCENTRATED

garlic FLAVOR HAS

SWEETENED THE BROTH,

THE SOUP IS ready

IN A FLASH.

3 quarts rich chicken broth
1 large head garlic, unpeeled
1 large sprig fresh epazote (optional)
2 fresh jalapeño peppers, stemmed
1 medium white onion, cut into
    $1/4$-inch dice
2 large, ripe tomatoes, cored,
    seeded, and cut into $1/4$-inch dice

Salt, about $1 1/2$ teaspoons, depending on
    the saltiness of the broth
$3/4$ cup loosely packed chopped cilantro
About 1 cup coarsely shredded cooked
    chicken (optional)
2 ripe avocados, peeled, pitted, and cut
    into $1/2$-inch dice
1 lime, cut into 6 to 8 wedges

✳ Pour the chicken broth into a large pot. Slice the unpeeled head of garlic in half width-wise and add both halves to the broth along with the optional epazote. Bring to a boil, reduce heat to medium-low, and simmer, partially covered, for about an hour. The liquid should have reduced to about 7 cups (almost by half). Remove the garlic and epazote, and discard.

✳ While the broth is simmering, cut the peppers in half lengthwise, cut out the seed pods, and slice into very thin lengthwise strips. Set aside with the diced onion and tomatoes.

✳ Generously season the broth with salt, then add the peppers and onion, partially cover, and simmer for 7 minutes. Add the tomatoes, cilantro, and optional chicken and simmer for 3 minutes, then ladle into warm bowls. Garnish with avocados, serve to your guests, and pass the lime wedges separately for each person to squeeze in to their liking. *Makes 8 cups*

VARIATION: Smoked chicken or other smoked poultry is delicious shredded into the soup. A little crème fraîche can be drizzled into the soup to make it richer.

French Peasant Soup

CLAIRE CRISCUOLO / REPRINTED FROM *CLAIRE'S CORNER COPIA COOKBOOK* **(PENGUIN BOOKS)**

4 quarts water
³/₄ pound Great Northern beans,
   picked over
1 small onion, chopped
8 cloves garlic, minced
¹/₂ cup olive oil
¹/₄ teaspoon dried thyme
1 bay leaf
¹/₄ teaspoon dried basil

6 carrots, cut into ¹/₂-inch pieces
4 celery stalks, trimmed and cut into
   ¹/₂-inch pieces
¹/₄ cup chopped fresh parsley
4 tablespoons (¹/₂ stick) butter
1 small head green cabbage, chopped
5 medium potatoes, diced
Salt and freshly ground black pepper

✻ In a large pot, bring water to a boil. Add the beans, reduce the heat to medium, and cook, uncovered, for 30 minutes, stirring frequently and skimming off any foam that rises to the top.

✻ Add the onions, garlic, olive oil, thyme, bay leaf, basil, carrots, celery, parsley, butter, and cabbage. Bring to a boil, reduce to a simmer, and simmer for 1½ hours, stirring frequently, until the beans are nearly tender.

✻ Add the potatoes, salt, and pepper and continue simmering for another 30 to 45 minutes, until the beans are very soft and the soup is thick. Adjust seasonings and serve hot.

SERVES 8

THIS IS A hearty, NUTRITIOUS, AND STEW-LIKE SOUP, WHICH IMPROVES IN flavor AS IT SITS IN THE REFRIGERATOR FOR A DAY OR TWO.

Bruschetta with Sweet Peppers and Ricotta

JANET FLETCHER / REPRINTED FROM *FRESH FROM THE FARMERS' MARKET* (CHRONICLE BOOKS)

SERVES 6

YOU MAY NEED TO

explore THE BREADS

AVAILABLE IN YOUR AREA

TO FIND THE IDEAL ONE

FOR bruschetta (PRO-

NOUNCED BREW-SKETTA).

IF THE BREAD IS TOO DENSE,

THE BRUSHETTA WILL BE

HARD TO eat; IF THE

BREAD HAS TOO MANY

HOLES, IT WON'T SUPPORT

THE topping. ONCE

TOASTED, THE BREAD

SHOULD BE sturdy

ENOUGH TO STAND UP TO

A SLATHERING OF PEPPERS

AND RICOTTA.

1 large red bell pepper
1 large golden bell pepper
1/4 cup extra-virgin olive oil
1 large clove of garlic, minced
Salt and freshly ground black pepper

6 slices country-style bread, each about
   1/4 inch thick and 4 inches long
1/2 pound whole-milk ricotta cheese
6 to 8 fresh basil leaves, torn into
   small pieces

✷ Roast peppers over a gas flame or charcoal fire, or under a broiler, until blackened on all sides. Transfer to a plastic bag. Close the bag so that peppers steam as they cool. When cool enough to handle, peel the peppers, halve them, and remove the seeds. Cut peppers into strips 1/4- to 1/2-inch wide.

✷ Heat 2 tablespoons of the olive oil in a skillet over medium heat. Add garlic and sauté until lightly colored, 1 to 2 minutes. Add peppers, season with salt and pepper to taste, and sauté until peppers are coated with oil and heated throughout. Remove from heat and cool in pan. For best flavor, sauté peppers 1 hour ahead so they can absorb the oil and exude their own juices.

✷ Toast the bread on both sides in a broiler, in a toaster oven, on a stove-top grill or—the best choice—over a charcoal fire. Remove from heat and drizzle one side of each slice with 1 teaspoon of olive oil.

✷ Season the ricotta cheese with salt and pepper and spread an even layer on each of the 6 toasts. Stir the basil into the peppers and divide the peppers and their juices among the 6 toasts. Serve hot.

Seviche

REPRINTED FROM *JOY OF COOKING* (SCRIBNER)

1 pound very fresh, firm-fleshed fish fillets
1/2 cup fresh lemon juice
1/2 cup fresh lime juice
1 cup tomato juice
1 1/2 tablespoons olive oil
1 medium, ripe tomato, cored and cut into
   1/4-inch dice
1 small onion, finely diced
1/4 cup pitted and coarsely chopped
   green olives

2 tablespoons chopped fresh cilantro
1 to 2 jalapeño peppers, seeded and
   minced
1 teaspoon dried oregano
1/2 teaspoon salt, or to taste
1/2 to 1 teaspoon sugar, or to taste

Fresh cilantro sprigs and diced avocado
   for garnish

✳ Remove all of the bones and skin from the fish. Cut the fish into small cubes, about ¾ inch each, and place in a glass or stainless steel mixing bowl. Stir in the lemon and lime juices. Cover with plastic wrap and refrigerate, stirring occasionally, until the fish is opaque throughout, 4 to 6 hours. (Break open a piece to test it.)

✳ Thoroughly drain the fish. (It can be refrigerated up to this point for 18 hours before serving, if desired.) To serve, mix the fish with the rest of the ingredients. Taste and adjust the seasonings and refrigerate until serving time. Serve in small bowls, garnished with cilantro sprigs and avocado.

SERVES 6

SEVICHE IS raw FISH MARINATED IN CITRUS JUICE. THOUGH THE FISH IS NOT technically COOKED, IT TURNS OPAQUE AND FIRMS UP SO THAT IT DOES NOT SEEM RAW. FISH OPTIONS FOR THIS DISH include GROUPER, HALIBUT, FLOUNDER, AND SNAPPER. BE SURE TO USE ONLY THE freshest OCEAN FISH AVAILABLE.

Smoked Salmon Napoleons

DENIS BLAIS, PACIFIC PALISADES HOTEL, VANCOUVER, BRITISH COLUMBIA

Pastry

4 sheets phyllo pastry
2 ounces clarified butter
2 tablespoons Parmesan cheese
2 tablespoons chopped fresh herbs (such as parsley, dill, tarragon, thyme)

Dressing

1/2 cup buttermilk
1/4 cup sour cream
1/4 cup mayonnaise
1 teaspoon horseradish

Juice of 2 lemons
2 tablespoons finely minced chives
2 tablespoons capers, drained
Salt and freshly ground black pepper to taste

1 cup radish sprouts, seeds cut off (mild arugula leaves can be substituted)
18 pieces smoked salmon (lox-style)
Extra chopped chives and drained capers for garnish

SERVES 6

CHEF DENIS BLAIS, ONE OF VANCOUVER'S premier CHEFS FROM THE MONTEREY BAR AND LOUNGE IN THE PACIFIC PALISADES HOTEL, picked THIS APPETIZER FOR BOTH ITS dazzling BEAUTY AND EASE OF PREPARATION.

✳ To make the pastry, brush 1 phyllo sheet with butter. Lightly sprinkle with a little cheese and herbs. Repeat procedure with each sheet, stacking one on top of another.

✳ Preheat the oven to 300°F. With a small, sharp knife, cut phyllo dough into 4 x 6-inch pieces (for a total of 24), placing each on a large baking sheet. Place in oven and bake for 7 to 8 minutes, until golden. Remove from oven and allow to cool.

✳ While pastry is baking, combine all of the dressing ingredients in a bowl and whisk thoroughly. Set aside.

✳ To finish, place 1 cooled phyllo square in the center of a plate. Put a small bunch of radish sprouts on top of it, then a drop of dressing, then 1 folded slice of smoked salmon; Repeat 3 more times, alternating sprouts, dressing, and salmon. Top with another phyllo square. Assemble 3 more Napoleons per plate, and pour dressing on plate surrounding Napoleons. Garnish with extra chives and capers.

Rice Paper–Wrapped Salad Rolls

MAI PHAM / REPRINTED FROM *THE BEST OF THAI AND VIETNAMESE COOKING*
(PRIMA PUBLISHING)

SERVES 6 TO 8

TRADITIONALLY filled
WITH juicy SHRIMP AND
PORK, THESE SALAD ROLLS
CAN ALSO BE stuffed
WITH GRILLED CHICKEN,
SALMON, OR TURKEY.

Salad Rolls

$1/2$ pound pork shoulder
12 medium-size raw shrimp with shells
8 (12-inch) round rice papers (keep extra
   on hand, in case you tear some)
1 small head red lettuce leaves, separated
   and washed
$1/4$ pound rice vermicelli, cooked in boiling
   water for 4 to 5 minutes, rinsed, and
   drained
1 cup bean sprouts
$1/2$ cup fresh mint leaves

Accompaniments

1 cup Hoisin-Peanut sauce (*see page 35*)
$1/4$ cup chopped roasted peanuts
2 tablespoons ground chili paste for
   garnish
Mint and cilantro sprigs for garnish
   (optional)

✱ In a small saucepan, cook pork shoulder in boiling salted water until just tender, about 30 minutes. Set aside to cool and then slice into 1 x 2½-inch pieces. Cook the shrimp in boiling salted water until just done, about 3 minutes, and drain. When cool enough to handle, shell, devein, and cut in half lengthwise. Refresh in cold water and set aside.

✱ Just before making the rolls, set up a salad roll "station." Fill a large mixing bowl with hot water. If necessary, keep some boiling water handy to add to the bowl if the temperature drops below 110°F. Choose an open area on the counter and arrange the following items in the order used: the rice paper, a damp cheesecloth, and a platter holding all the stuffing ingredients.

✱ Working with only 2 rice paper sheets at a time, dip 1 sheet, edge first, in the hot water and turn it completely, about 10 seconds. Lay the sheet down on the cheesecloth and stretch the edges slightly to remove any wrinkles. Wet the other rice paper the same way and place it alongside the first.

✱ Line the bottom third of the wet, pliable rice sheet with 3 shrimp halves, cut side up, and top with two slices of the pork. Make sure the ingredients are neatly placed in a straight row. Fold a piece of lettuce into a thin rectangle about 5 inches long and place it on top. (You may need to use only half of a leaf.) Next, top with about 1 tablespoon of vermicelli, 1 tablespoon bean sprouts, and 4 to 5 mint leaves. Make sure the ingredients are not clumped together in the center, but evenly distributed from one end to the other, leaving an inch or so on each end without filling.

✱ Using your second, third, and fourth fingers, press down on the ingredients while you use the other hand to fold over both sides of the rice paper. (Pressing down on the ingredients is particularly important because it tightens the roll.) With fingers still pressing down, use both thumbs to fold the bottom edge over the filling and roll into a cylinder about 1½ inches wide by 5 inches long. Finish making all the remaining rolls.

✱ To serve, cut the rolls into 2 or 4 equal pieces and place the cut rolls upright on an appetizer plate. Serve with Hoisin-Peanut Sauce on the side. Top with chopped peanuts and chili paste. If you like, garnish the rolls with mint or cilantro sprigs.

Hoisin-Peanut Sauce

1 cup hoisin sauce
½ cup water
¼ cup rice wine vinegar
⅓ cup puréed or finely minced yellow onion

1 tablespoon ground chili paste, or to taste
1 tablespoon chopped roasted peanuts for garnish

✱ In a small saucepan, place first 4 ingredients and bring to a boil, stirring to combine. Reduce heat and let simmer for 5 to 7 minutes. Sauce should be thick enough to coat the back of a spoon and have a syrup-like consistency. Add a little water if sauce is too thick.

✱ Transfer mixture to a sauce dish and garnish with chili paste and chopped peanuts.

MAKES 2 CUPS

WITH THE addition OF CHOPPED GARLIC, GINGER, AND CHILIES, THIS SAUCE CAN also BE USED ON GRILLED CHICKEN, FISH, OR BEEF. IT'S ALSO wonderful AS A MARINADE.

Grilled Ratatouille

CHRIS JOHNSON, EXECUTIVE CHEF, RAINCITY GRILL, VANCOUVER, BRITISH COLUMBIA

Basil Pesto
1/4 cup basil leaves
1/4 cup pine nuts
1/4 cup olive oil
2 cloves garlic, peeled
1 teaspoon lemon juice

Roasted Garlic
3 whole heads garlic
Olive oil
Salt and freshly ground black pepper

Reduced Balsamic Vinegar Sauce
1 1/2 cups balsamic vinegar

1 small eggplant, trimmed to 3 inches and
cut into 1/4-inch slices
1 small zucchini, trimmed to 3 inches and
cut into 1/4-inch slices
1 yellow bell pepper, cored, seeded, and
cut into 6 wedges
1 red bell pepper, cored, seeded, and
cut into 6 wedges
3 large Roma tomatoes, cut in half
Salt and freshly ground black pepper
6 tablespoons crumbled feta cheese

SERVES 6

RATATOUILLE shaken up AND PUT BACK TOGETHER IN A WHOLE new WAY.

✷ To make pesto, place basil, pine nuts, olive oil, garlic, and lemon juice in a food processor or blender. Blend until smooth. Set aside.

✷ To make roasted garlic, preheat oven to 350°F. Cut off tops of heads of garlic. Drizzle tops of exposed garlic with a little olive oil and sprinkle with salt and pepper. Wrap in aluminum foil and bake for around 45 minutes. Remove from oven and when cool enough to handle, pop individual cloves from head. Set aside.

✷ To make reduced balsamic vinegar sauce, place vinegar in a medium saucepan and bring to a simmer. Simmer, uncovered, to reduce by two-thirds, about ½ hour. Set aside.

✷ Start fire or turn gas grill to medium hot.

✷ Place eggplant, zucchini, peppers, and tomatoes in a large bowl. Season with salt and pepper and toss again. Place on a medium-hot fire and grill for 2 to 3 minutes per side. Remove from grill.

✷ On 6 individual serving plates, arrange the vegetables. Start with a slice of eggplant, followed by a red pepper wedge and another slice of eggplant. Follow with 2 pieces of zucchini and then a yellow pepper wedge. Top with a tomato half. (The vegetables are warm and can be gently pushed together.)

✷ Drizzle basil pesto over the vegetables and lightly over plate. Drizzle the plate with reduced balsamic vinegar sauce. Sprinkle with roasted garlic cloves and feta cheese and serve.

Villager's Leek and Fennel Pie

DIANE KOCHILAS / REPRINTED FROM *THE GREEK VEGETARIAN* (ST. MARTIN'S PRESS)

SERVES 6 TO 8

DIANE traveled EXTENSIVELY THROUGHOUT GREECE AND DISCOVERED MANY authentic AND DELICIOUS DISHES LIKE THIS ONE, WHICH IS PERFUMED WITH THE aromas OF FENNEL AND LEEK.

YOU WILL also HAVE EXCELLENT RESULTS WITH frozen PHYLLO DOUGH.

Homemade Phyllo Dough

4 to 4^1/$_2$ cups all-purpose flour
1 scant teaspoon salt
1^1/$_2$ to 1^3/$_4$ cups warm water
^{1}/$_4$ cup olive oil
2 tablespoons red wine vinegar or strained
   fresh lemon juice

NOTE: Make dough at least 2 hours
before assembling pie

Filling

^{1}/$_2$ cup extra-virgin olive oil, plus oil
   for phyllo
2 large leeks, whites and green, trimmed,
   washed, and coarsely chopped
2 medium fennel bulbs, trimmed, halved,
   and coarsely chopped
1 cup chopped fresh dill
1 cup crumbled feta cheese
1 to 2 eggs
Salt and freshly ground black pepper
Grating (or pinch) of nutmeg

* To make homemade phyllo dough: Combine 4 cups of the flour and salt in a large mixing bowl and make a well in the center. Add the water, olive oil, and vinegar. Work the flour into the liquid with a fork, until a dough begins to form, then knead it in the bowl, adding a little more flour if necessary. The dough should be silky, pliant, and smooth. Cover and let rest at room temperature for at least 2 hours before using. (Dough can also be made in a stand mixer with a dough hook.)

* In a large skillet, heat 3 tablespoons of the olive oil. Add leeks and fennel and sauté over medium heat until pearly, about 7 minutes.

* In a large mixing bowl, combine the sautéed leeks and fennel with the dill, feta, remaining olive oil, and 1 egg. Mix well. If the mixture seems too dry, add the other egg. Season with salt, pepper, and nutmeg and toss again.

* Preheat oven to 350°F. With 1 teaspoon of olive oil, oil a 9 x 1-inch round baking dish. Divide the dough into 4 equal balls. Lightly flour a surface and roll out the first dough ball to a circle slightly larger than the circumference of the pan. Place the phyllo in the pan and oil it with 1 teaspoon of olive oil. Repeat with second dough ball. Spread the filling on top. Roll out the third ball of dough, oil it, and place it on top of the filling, and repeat with last ball. Pinch the bottom and top phyllo sheets together and roll inward to form the rim of the crust. Make two incisions with a sharp paring knife in the top of the dough. Bake for about 1 hour, or until the phyllo is golden. Remove, cool, and serve.

Knecht Burgers

JAMES MCNAIR / REPRINTED FROM *JAMES MCNAIR'S BURGERS* (CHRONICLE BOOKS)

1 1/2 pounds ground lean beef
1/4 cup finely chopped yellow onion
2 tablespoons Worcestershire sauce, or
    to taste
Salt

1 sweet French or Italian baguette, about
    2 1/2 inches wide, split lengthwise
Unsalted butter, softened, for spreading
Yellow American or Dijon-style mustard

✳ In a large bowl, combine the beef, onion, Worcestershire sauce, and salt to taste.

✳ Preheat the oven to 400°F. Spread the bread with a thin coating of the butter. Spread the meat mixture over the bread in an even layer about 1/4 inch thick. Be sure that the meat covers the edges of the bread; any exposed bread will burn. Press the meat down around the edges with a fork or your fingers to adhere it to the bread. Spread a thin layer of mustard over the meat. Place the bread on an ungreased baking sheet.

✳ Place burgers in the hot oven and cook until done to preference, about 6 to 7 minutes for medium-rare.

✳ Transfer the baguette halves to a cutting surface and cut each piece crosswise into 8 equal sections, or as desired.

SERVES 8

THE PROBLEM WITH THESE SAVORY mini-burger APPETIZERS IS THAT THEY DISAPPEAR FASTER THAN YOU CAN MAKE THEM. THE SOLUTION? MAKE scores OF THEM AHEAD OF TIME AND FREEZE.

Chili Cheesecake

LORA BRODY / REPRINTED FROM *PLUGGED IN* (WILLIAM MORROW AND COMPANY)

MAKES ONE

10-INCH CAKE

THIS COMBINATION OF

smooth CREAM

CHEESE LACED WITH THE

ZING OF CHILI MAKES FOR

A NEW TAKE ON A first

COURSE OR APPETIZER.

SERVE WITH CRACKERS OR

sturdy TORTILLA CHIPS.

Butter for greasing pan
Corn chips to equal 1 1/2 cups of very
  fine crumbs
1/3 cup butter
2 pounds cream cheese at room temperature (don't use whipped cream cheese)
1/3 cup heavy cream
4 extra-large eggs
2 teaspoons mild chili powder

1 or 2 chipotle (smoked jalapeño) peppers,
  minced (depending upon the desired
  heat)
1 cup smoked Gouda cheese,
  shredded or grated
1 medium onion, coarsely chopped and
  sautéed in 3 tablespoons butter
1/2 cup cilantro, finely chopped
1/3 cup very lean smoked ham, minced

✱ Preheat the oven to 300°F with the rack in the center position. Butter a 10-inch layer pan with 3-inch sides. Grind corn chips in a food processor until very fine. Add the butter and pulse a couple of times. Use this mixture to coat the bottom and halfway up the sides of the pan.

✱ Place the cream cheese, cream, eggs, chili powder, and peppers into the food processor and process until completely mixed. Add the last 4 ingredients and pulse a few times to incorporate. (Do not process to a smooth consistency.)

✱ Pour the batter into the prepared pan, shake to level the top, and set the pan in a large roasting pan. Add hot water to the depth of 2 inches up the side of the cake pan.

✱ Place in oven and bake for 1 hour and 45 minutes. At the end of this time turn off the oven, but let the cake remain in the oven with the door closed for 1 more hour. Remove the pan to a counter and let rest for at least 1 hour more or until completely cool. Do not refrigerate.

Spaghettini with Red and Gold Cherry Tomatoes

JANET FLETCHER / REPRINTED FROM *FRESH FROM THE FARMERS' MARKET* **(CHRONICLE BOOKS)**

1/4 pound sweet red cherry tomatoes, halved

1/4 pound small golden cherry tomatoes, halved

3 large shallots, minced

1/4 cup extra-virgin olive oil

Scant 1/4 teaspoon hot red pepper flakes

Salt and freshly ground black pepper

1 pound dried spaghetti

1/2 cup loosely packed fresh basil leaves, stacked a few at a time and cut into thin ribbons

✳ In a large saucepan, combine tomatoes, shallots, olive oil, hot pepper flakes, and salt and pepper to taste. Bring to a simmer over medium heat and simmer until tomatoes render their juices, about 5 minutes. Remove from the heat before the tomatoes completely collapse and lose their shape.

✳ Bring a large pot of salted water to a boil over high heat. Add pasta and cook until al dente. Just before pasta is done, reheat sauce gently. Add basil leaves to sauce. Taste and adjust seasonings.

✳ Drain pasta and return to pot. Add sauce and toss well. Serve on warm plates.

SERVES 4 TO 6

WHEN THE INGREDIENTS ARE FARM-FRESH, EVEN THE simplest OF PASTA DISHES STANDS OUT. THE sauce CAN BE MADE WITH RED TOMATOES ALONE, BUT THE gold TOMATOES ADD EYE APPEAL.

Orecchiette with Endive and Sun-Dried Tomatoes

ROZANNE GOLD / REPRINTED FROM *RECIPES 1-2-3* (VIKING PENGUIN)

One 8-ounce jar sun-dried tomatoes in oil
³/₄ pound (about 3 medium) endive
Salt and freshly ground black pepper

8 ounces orecchiette pasta
1 tablespoon small capers

✳ Drain the oil from the tomatoes and place oil in a large skillet. Cut the tomatoes in half and add them to the oil. Slice the endive into ¼-inch-thick slices (hold the knife on the diagonal to make oval-shaped slices). Add to the oil. Cook over medium-high heat until the endive is soft and the tomatoes are tender, about 10 minutes. Add salt and freshly ground black pepper to taste.

✳ Meanwhile, cook the pasta for 12 to 15 minutes in boiling, salted water or until done. Drain well. Put the pasta on a warm platter and cover thoroughly with sauce. Sprinkle with capers. Serve hot, or cold as a salad.

SERVES 4

SUN-DRIED TOMATOES
marinated IN OLIVE
OIL ARE A GOOD ADDITION
TO ANY pantry FOR
QUICK-FIX MEALS.
ORECCHIETTE IS pasta
SHAPED LIKE LITTLE EARS.

Roasted Red Pepper Spread

BARBARA KAFKA / REPRINTED FROM *ROASTING* (WILLIAM MORROW AND COMPANY)

Two 7-ounce jars roasted red peppers,
    drained
2 tablespoons extra-virgin olive oil
2 tablespoons minced fresh Italian
    parsley leaves

1 tablespoon fresh lemon juice
2 teaspoons capers, drained
1 medium clove garlic, smashed,
    peeled, and mashed to a paste with
    a pinch of salt

✳ Arrange the drained peppers on a double layer of paper towels and let them dry while preparing the recipe.

✳ Combine the remaining ingredients in the work bowl of a food processor. Process until the capers are very finely chopped. (This can also be done by hand with a chef's knife.) Add the drained peppers and pulse (or chop) until peppers are coarsely chopped. Stop several times to scrape down the sides of the work bowl to make sure the mixture is evenly chopped. Check the seasonings and adjust as necessary.

✳ Store the spread in a covered container in the refrigerator for up to 5 days. Remove to room temperature at least 30 minutes before serving.

MAKES 2 CUPS

THIS RECIPE IS easily
MULTIPLIED USING JARRED
RED PEPPERS AND WILL
keep FOR UP TO 5 DAYS
IN THE REFRIGERATOR. IT
IS GOOD served WITH
VEGETABLE CRUDITÉS AND
ON crostini.

MAKES 1¹/₄ CUPS

A PROVENÇAL-STYLE OLIVE

PASTE, tapenade HAS

FOUND A PERMANENT

PLACE IN America's

CONDIMENT CABINET.

MAKES 1¹/₄ CUPS

A PROVENÇAL-STYLE OLIVE

PASTE, tapenade HAS

FOUND A PERMANENT

PLACE IN America's

CONDIMENT CABINET.

SERVES 8

THIS puréed BEAN

RECIPE CAN BE USED FOR

DIPPING CORN CHIPS OR

spread ONTO WHOLE-

GRAIN BREADS.

Black Olive Tapenade

ROZANNE GOLD / REPRINTED FROM *RECIPES 1-2-3* (VIKING PENGUIN)

2 cups pitted, oil-cured black olives
One 2-ounce can anchovies with capers,
   drained and patted dry

¹/₄ cup fruity olive oil
Freshly ground black pepper

✳ Put the olives and anchovies with capers in a food processor or blender. With the motor running, slowly add the oil until the tapenade is smooth: add an extra tablespoon of oil if necessary. Add freshly ground black pepper to taste.

Roasted Garlic and Bean Spread with Crusty Bread

JAMES MCNAIR / REPRINTED FROM *JAMES MCNAIR'S BEANS & GRAINS* (CHRONICLE BOOKS)

1 cup dried small white beans, such as
   cannelloni or flageolets (*see cooking
   directions for dried beans on page 47*)
   or 2 cups canned small white beans
2 or 3 whole heads garlic
Olive oil, preferably extra-virgin

Salt
Freshly ground black pepper
Fresh flat-leaf parsley for garnish
Sliced whole-grain French- or
   Italian-style bread

✳ If using dried beans, cook the beans according to the directions on page 47.

✳ To roast the garlic, preheat the oven to 350°F. Slice the heads horizontally, cutting away the top one-fourth to expose individual cloves. Peel away the outer papery skin, leaving the garlic heads intact. Place in a small baking dish, rub generously with olive oil, and sprinkle with salt. Cover tightly with aluminum foil and bake for 45 minutes. Uncover and roast until completely soft, about 15 minutes longer. Remove from the oven and set aside. When cool enough to handle, squeeze the garlic from the skin into a small bowl.

✳ Drain the beans and transfer 2 cups to a food processor or blender. (Cover and refrigerate or freeze any remaining beans for another purpose.) Add the roasted garlic and blend until fairly smooth. Season to taste with olive oil, salt, and pepper. Transfer to a small crock, garnish with parsley, and serve with sliced bread. *Makes 2 cups*

SIDES & SALADS

Tuscan Salad of Chicory, White Beans, and Hearts of Palm

CLAIRE CRISCUOLO / REPRINTED FROM *CLAIRE'S CLASSIC VEGETARIAN COOKING* (DUTTON)

1 medium head of chicory, cut into bite-size pieces

1 head of endive, cut into bite-size pieces

1 small head radicchio, cut into bite-size pieces

4 radishes, thinly sliced

1/2 small cucumber, peeled, seeded, and diced

7 ounces canned hearts of palm, drained and cut into 1/4-inch slices

1 cup freshly cooked or canned white beans, drained (*see cooking directions for dried beans below*)

1/2 small, sweet onion, sliced thinly

2 large cloves garlic, minced

3 tablespoons extra-virgin olive oil

1 lemon, squeezed (about 4 tablespoons juice)

Salt and freshly ground black pepper

SERVES 8

THE gourmet OR IMPORT SECTIONS OF MOST SUPERMARKETS CARRY hearts OF PALM PACKED IN CANS OR JARS.

✳ Place the chicory, endive, radicchio, radishes, cucumber, hearts of palm, beans, onion, and garlic in a large salad bowl. Toss well using two spoons. Drizzle the olive oil evenly over the salad. Toss to coat the leaves evenly. Drizzle the lemon juice over the salad. Toss well to mix evenly. Add salt and pepper to taste. Toss again to mix well.

NOTE: To cook dried beans, carefully pick through beans to remove any foreign bits or imperfect beans. Place in a large bowl and cover with water by 3 inches. Let stand for several hours or, preferably, overnight.

Drain beans, rinse, and drain again. Transfer beans to a large heavy-bottomed pot. Add enough water to cover by about 1 inch and stir well. Bring to a boil. Using a wire skimmer or slotted utensil, remove any foam that rises to the surface.

Boil for 10 minutes, reduce heat to a gentle simmer, and cover partially. Simmer for 45 minutes to 1½ hours, until beans are tender but still hold their shape.

Green Bean Salad with Cherry Tomatoes and Ricotta Salata

JANET FLETCHER / REPRINTED FROM *FRESH FROM THE FARMERS' MARKET* (CHRONICLE BOOKS)

Dressing

1/4 cup extra-virgin olive oil

1 tablespoon plus 2 teaspoons white wine vinegar

Salt and freshly ground black pepper

1/2 red onion, thinly sliced

Ice water

1 pound thin green beans (*haricots verts*), trimmed

1/2 pound small cherry tomatoes (preferably red and gold varieties mixed), halved

2 ounces ricotta salata cheese

✳ To make the dressing, whisk together olive oil, vinegar, and salt and pepper in a large bowl. (Beans need a lot of salt.) Whisk in onion and set dressing aside.

✳ Have ready a bowl of ice water. Bring a large pot of salted water to a boil over high heat. Add beans and cook until crisp-tender, about 5 minutes. Drain in a colander or sieve, then transfer beans to the ice water to stop cooking. When beans are cool, drain again and pat thoroughly dry with a clean dish towel.

✳ Add beans to bowl with dressing and toss to coat. Add tomatoes and toss again. With a cheese plane, shave the cheese directly into the bowl in paper-thin slices. Toss again gently to keep the flakes in large pieces, then transfer salad to a shallow serving platter.

SERVES 6

TENDER, SWEET, AND DELICATE, THE elegant GREEN FILET BEANS (ALSO KNOWN AS *HARICOTS VERTS*) deserve TO BE THE CENTERPIECE OF A summer MEAL. IF YOU CAN'T find RICOTTA SALATA—A SLICEABLE ITALIAN SHEEP'S MILK CHEESE—USE GREEK manouri OR ANY YOUNG SHEEP'S MILK CHEESE FIRM ENOUGH TO SHAVE INTO PALE flakes WITH A CHEESE PLANE.

Roasted Root Vegetable Slaw with Gingered Apples, Raisins, Walnuts and Barley

MARCEL DESAULNIERS / REPRINTED FROM *SALAD DAYS* (WILLIAM MORROW AND COMPANY)

SERVES 4

KEEP IN mind THAT THIS RECIPE, ALTHOUGH LENGTHY, IS AN ENTIRE meal AND DEFINITELY WELL WORTH THE EFFORT. IT CAN BE BROKEN DOWN INTO SEVERAL stages, WHICH CAN BE MADE WELL IN ADVANCE OF THE FINAL assembly OF THE SALAD BEFORE SERVING.

Gingered Apples, Raisins, and Walnuts

$1/2$ cup walnuts
1 cup port wine
1 teaspoon fresh lemon juice
1 Granny Smith apple, unpeeled
1 Red Delicious apple, unpeeled
1 tablespoon safflower oil
$3/4$ cup finely diced onion
$1/4$ cup finely diced celery
Salt and freshly ground black pepper
$1/2$ cup raisins
2 tablespoons cider vinegar
1 teaspoon grated fresh ginger

Brown Mustard Dressing

6 tablespoons spicy brown mustard
6 tablespoons pure apple juice
3 tablespoons mayonnaise
$1^1/2$ tablespoons cider vinegar
Salt and freshly ground black pepper

Root Vegetable Slaw

1 medium rutabaga, ends trimmed, peeled, and cut into strips 3 inches x $1/8$ inch
2 medium carrots, ends trimmed, peeled, and cut into strips 2 inches x $1/8$ inch
4 tablespoons safflower oil
2 small turnips, ends trimmed, peeled, and cut into strips 3 inches x $1/8$ inch
2 medium parsnips, ends trimmed, peeled, and cut into strips 3 inches x $1/8$ inch
Salt and freshly ground black pepper
$1/2$ cup Brown Mustard Dressing

Apple and Rosemary-Scented Barley

6 cups pure apple juice
1 teaspoon salt
1 teaspoon chopped fresh rosemary
$1^1/2$ cups pearl barley

$1/2$ pound washed and dried green leaf lettuce

✳ To make the gingered apples, raisins, and walnuts: Preheat the oven to 325°F. Toast the walnuts on a baking sheet in the oven for 10 minutes, or until lightly golden and fragrant, shaking pan occasionally. Cool the nuts and chop coarsely.

✳ Heat the port in a medium saucepan over medium-high heat. Bring to a boil, lower heat, and simmer, uncovered, for 15 minutes or until reduced to about 2 tablespoons. Remove from heat and set aside.

✳ In a nonreactive bowl, add the lemon juice to 2 quarts of cold water. Core and quarter the apples, then cut into $1/4$-inch slices. Immediately place the apple slices in the water to prevent them from discoloring.

✳ Heat the 1 tablespoon of safflower oil in a large nonstick pan over medium heat. When oil is hot, add the onions and celery. Season with salt and pepper and cook, stirring, for 3 minutes.

✳ Drain the apples in a colander, rinse under cold water, and shake dry. Add to onion-celery mixture along with the raisins and the 2 tablespoons of cider vinegar and continue to cook, stirring occasionally, for 2 minutes. Add the ginger, stir to combine, and cook for 1 minute.

✳ Remove the pan from the heat, add the walnuts and port wine reduction. Stir to combine. Transfer to a nonreactive bowl and set aside, uncovered, at room temperature for up to 4 hours before serving. (Or cool to room temperature and refrigerate in a nonreactive, covered container for up to 4 days before serving.)

✳ To make the brown mustard dressing: In a nonreactive bowl, whisk together the mustard, 6 tablespoons of the apple juice, the mayonnaise, and the 1½ tablespoons cider vinegar until smooth. Adjust the seasonings with salt and pepper and whisk to combine. Cover tightly with plastic wrap and refrigerate until ready to serve. *Makes 1 cup*

✳ To make the root vegetable slaw: Preheat the oven to 375°F. Place the rutabaga and carrot strips in a large, nonreactive bowl with 2 tablespoons of the safflower oil. Season to taste with the salt and pepper and stir to coat the vegetables with the oil. Transfer to a nonstick baking sheet. Spread out into a single layer covering the pan and set aside.

✳ Repeat the above process with the turnips and parsnips and place on a separate baking sheet.

✳ Place the baking sheets in the preheated oven. Roast the rutabagas and carrots for 10 minutes and the turnips and parsnips for 15 minutes. Cool the vegetables at room temperature for 30 minutes.

✳ Transfer the root vegetables to a large, nonreactive bowl, add ½ cup of the brown mustard dressing and use a rubber spatula to combine. Cover bowl tightly with plastic wrap and refrigerate for up to 2 days before serving.

✳ To make the apple and rosemary-scented barley: Heat the 6 cups of apple juice with 1 teaspoon of the salt and rosemary in a large saucepan over medium-high heat. When the juice boils, add the barley. Return to a boil, reduce to a simmer, and simmer for 45 minutes until barley is tender but not mushy.

✳ Drain the barley and then cool with cold water. Drain well and transfer barley to a large, nonreactive bowl. Cover tightly with plastic wrap and refrigerate for up to 2 days before serving.

✳ To assemble the salad: Divide and arrange the lettuce onto 4 dinner plates. Arrange an equal amount of the barley on each plate, on top of the lettuce. Dress each plate with 2 tablespoons of the brown mustard dressing and place an equal amount of the root vegetable slaw in the middle of the barley on each plate. Portion an equal amount of gingered apples, raisins, and walnuts in the middle of the slaw on each plate. Serve immediately.

Grilled Caesar Salad

CHRIS JOHNSON, EXECUTIVE CHEF, RAINCITY GRILL, VANCOUVER, BRITISH COLUMBIA

Lemon Preserve

2 lemons, quartered, seeded, and each
   quarter cut into $1/8$-inch slices
4 cups water
$1/3$ cup sugar
$1/2$ cup white wine vinegar

Fried Capers and Caper Oil

1 cup canola oil
6 tablespoons medium capers, rinsed and
   patted dry

Salad

3 heads Romaine lettuce
$1^{1}/2$ cups of your favorite bottled Caesar
   dressing
2 cups toasted croutons
6 tablespoons grated Parmesan cheese

✱ To make lemon preserve, place lemon slices in a small saucepan with 2 cups of the water. Bring to a simmer and simmer for 20 minutes. Drain, and return lemon slices to saucepan. Add remaining 2 cups of water, sugar, and vinegar, and bring to a simmer, stirring to dissolve sugar. Simmer another 20 minutes, stirring often. Remove from heat and allow to cool.

✱ To make fried capers and caper oil, heat oil in a medium-size saucepan over medium-high heat. Add capers and cook until capers open. Remove capers with a slotted spoon and drain on paper towels. Set caper oil aside.

✱ Start a fire or turn on gas grill to medium high.

✱ Cut lettuce in half lengthwise, keeping stem intact, to create two open pieces held together by stem. Square off tops of lettuce pieces with a sharp knife. Place lettuce pieces, cut side down, over fire, and cook for about 2 minutes—the lettuce should be browned without turning black or burning. Turn and repeat on other side.

✱ Remove lettuce from grill and cut out connecting stem, creating 6 grilled pieces of lettuce. Place, cut side up, on serving plates.

✱ Drizzle 1 tablespoon of lemon preserve over each piece of lettuce, followed by 1 tablespoon of fried capers. Drizzle a teaspoon of caper oil over tops of salads. Drizzle about 4 tablespoons of Caesar dressing over each plate, followed by $1/3$ cup of croutons and 1 tablespoon of cheese, and serve.

Shredded Chicken Salad with Spicy Sesame Vinaigrette

STEVEN WONG / REPRINTED FROM *NEW WORLD NOODLES* **(ROBERT ROSE)**

SERVES 4

THIS IS A tasty WAY TO STRETCH LEFTOVER ROAST CHICKEN OR TURKEY. IN FACT, ROAST BEEF OR PORK WILL DO JUST AS well.

Dressing
2 tablespoons honey
1 tablespoon Worcestershire sauce
1 1/2 cups Spicy Sesame Vinaigrette
    (*see below*)

Salad
2 cups bean sprouts (preferably mung bean)
2 tablespoons vegetable oil
3 cloves garlic, peeled and very thinly
    sliced lengthwise

1 pound Chinese-style steamed noodles or
    8 ounces dried fettuccine
1 cup English cucumber, cut into thin
    matchsticks
1 cup carrots, cut into thin matchsticks
2 cups cooked chicken, beef, or pork,
    cut into julienne strips
1/2 cup thinly sliced green onions, green
    parts only
2 tablespoons sesame seeds

✳ In a small bowl or pot, combine all dressing ingredients and mix well. (If necessary, warm dressing over low heat or in a microwave to ensure honey is dissolved.)

✳ In a large bowl of ice water, refresh bean sprouts for 15 minutes until crisp. Drain and set aside.

✳ In a small skillet, heat oil over medium heat for 30 seconds. Add garlic and fry until light golden, about 2 minutes. (Be careful not to let it burn.) With a slotted spoon, remove garlic slices and discard. Reserve oil.

✳ In a large pot of boiling salted water, blanch noodles for 1 minute. Drain and, using chopsticks or two forks, toss to dry. (If using pasta, prepare according to package directions.) Transfer to a large salad bowl, toss with reserved garlic oil, and allow to cool.

✳ Add bean sprouts, cucumber, carrots, chicken, and green onions to noodles. Pour dressing evenly over salad; toss well. Sprinkle with sesame seeds and serve immediately.

Spicy Sesame Vinaigrette

1/2 cup soy sauce
1/2 cup Chinese red vinegar or balsamic
    vinegar
1 tablespoon sesame oil

1 tablespoon chili oil or 1 to 2 jalapeño
    peppers, thinly sliced
1 tablespoon minced fresh ginger
2 tablespoons water or chicken stock

✳ In a small bowl, combine all of the ingredients. Set aside for 30 minutes to develop flavors. Serve at room temperature. *Makes about 1 1/2 cups*

Soothing Summer Turkey Salad

BARBARA KAFKA / REPRINTED FROM *ROASTING* (WILLIAM MORROW AND COMPANY)

1 cucumber, peeled, cut in half lengthwise, seeded, and cut across into $1/4$-inch pieces

2 small tomatoes, cored and cut in $1/2$-inch cubes

$2^1/2$ teaspoons kosher salt

$3/4$ pound of 1-inch cubed roast turkey meat (about 2 cups)

2 scallions, trimmed and white and green parts cut into $1/2$-inch pieces

3 to 4 radishes, trimmed and sliced into very thin rounds

2 tablespoons chopped fresh dill

Freshly ground black pepper to taste

✱ Place cucumber and tomatoes in a medium bowl. Add salt and toss. Add the rest of the ingredients and toss gently. Let sit for 10 to 15 minutes at room temperature to allow flavors to develop. Serve on a bed of crisp lettuce greens.

SERVES 6 TO 8

A LIGHT AND REFRESHING WARM weather MEAL, WHICH CAN BE MADE IN minutes.

Latin-Flavored Coleslaw with Grilled Avocados

CHRIS SCHLESINGER AND JOHN WILLOUGHBY/ REPRINTED FROM *LICENSE TO GRILL* **(WILLIAM MORROW AND COMPANY)**

Dressing

3/4 cup mayonnaise

1/3 cup olive oil

1/3 cup fresh lime juice (about 2 large limes)

1/4 cup red wine vinegar

2 ears husked corn, blanched in boiling salted water for 2 minutes, drained and kernels cut from cob (about 1 cup kernels)

2 tablespoons sugar

2 tablespoons catsup

4 to 10 dashes Tabasco sauce, to taste

Salt and freshly ground black pepper to taste

Coleslaw

2 cups shredded green cabbage

1 cup shredded red cabbage

1 cup shredded carrots (about 1 medium carrot)

3 ripe but firm avocados, halved and pitted, but not peeled

2 tablespoons olive oil

1 tablespoon chili powder

1 tablespoon ground cumin

Salt and freshly ground black pepper

✳ To make the dressing: In a food processor or blender, combine all the dressing ingredients and purée until smooth.

✳ In a medium bowl, combine the green cabbage, red cabbage, and carrots. Add the dressing, mix well, cover, and refrigerate.

✳ Start fire.

✳ Sprinkle the avocado with the olive oil, chili powder, cumin, and salt and pepper to taste. Place them on the grill over a medium-hot fire, cut side down, and cook for 3 to 5 minutes, or until seared. Pull the avocados off the grill and, as soon as they are cool enough to handle, turn them out of their skins, slice them, and serve them on top of generous helpings of the slaw. (If the avocados don't slip out of their skins easily, just spoon out chunks on top of the slaw.)

SERVES 4 TO 6

AIDED BY THE chili POWDER AND CUMIN, THE CUT SIDE OF THE avocado SHOULD ACQUIRE A WELL-SEARED AND flavorful COATING. RIPE BUT FIRM IS THE ideal TEXTURE FOR THE AVOCADO, BUT YOU CAN GET AWAY WITH VERY FIRM OR MUSHY; anything BUT ROCK HARD.

Asian Coleslaw

LORA BRODY / REPRINTED FROM *PLUGGED IN* (WILLIAM MORROW AND COMPANY, INC.)

Dressing
1 cup mayonnaise
1 teaspoon red wine vinegar
Zest of 1 orange
2 tablespoons orange juice
1/4 teaspoon sesame seed oil
2 tablespoons soy sauce
Salt to taste

Coleslaw
1 medium cabbage, cored, quartered and
    cut to fit the tube of a food processor
1 small jicama, peeled
1 medium red onion, peeled and quartered
1 orange, peeled, seeded, and sectioned

✳ Add the dressing ingredients to a food processor fitted with a metal blade. Process until smooth, about 10 to 12 seconds. Pour dressing into a large bowl.

✳ Without washing bowl of food processor, remove metal blade and replace with a shredding disc. Shred the cabbage and jicama and add to the dressing.

✳ Remove the shredding disc and replace with a fine or medium slicing disc. Using the large feed tube, slice the red onion. Add the onion slices and orange sections to the bowl with dressing and cabbage. Toss gently to coat all ingredients with the dressing. *Makes 5 cups*

SERVES 8 TO 10

THIS colorful VARIA-
TION ON THE COLESLAW
theme FEATURES CON-
TRASTING COLORS AND
TEXTURES OF RED ONION,
MANDARIN oranges,
JICAMA, AND CABBAGE.

Cabbage Salad with Prosciutto

GEORGEANNE BRENNAN / REPRINTED FROM *THE FOOD AND FLAVORS OF HAUTE PROVENCE* (CHRONICLE BOOKS)

2 1/2 cups shredded cabbage (a food
    processor fitted with a shredding disc
    works well)
1/4 cup extra-virgin olive oil
3 tablespoons red wine vinegar

1 tablespoon Dijon mustard
1/2 teaspoon salt
5 very thin slices prosciutto
1/2 teaspoon freshly ground black pepper

✳ In a large mixing bowl, toss together all of the ingredients except the black pepper. When well blended, stir in the pepper and remove to a serving bowl.

SERVES 3 TO 4

AN EXAMPLE OF simple
INGREDIENTS COMBINED
WITH A simple
PREPARATION CREATING
A COMMANDING dish.

Home-Style Stuffed Artichokes

TOM LACALAMITA / REPRINTED FROM *THE ULTIMATE PRESSURE COOKER COOKBOOK* **(SIMON & SCHUSTER)**

4 large artichokes (approximately 8 to 10 ounces each), untrimmed
2 large eggs
¼ cup Pecorino-Romano cheese
1 clove garlic, peeled and minced
1 tablespoon minced parsley

Pinch of freshly ground black pepper
1 cup water
1 teaspoon salt
1 bay leaf
2 tablespoons extra-virgin olive oil

✳ Remove stems from the artichokes with a sharp knife. Tear off and discard the top 2 or 3 layers of tough outer leaves. Trim the base so that the artichokes stand flat. Cut off ½ to 1 inch from the tops of the artichokes. Carefully open the center of the artichoke to expose the center leaves and choke. Pull out and remove any thorny leaves, which are usually tinged with purple. With a teaspoon, scoop out and discard any fuzzy matter from the center choke. Set aside.

✳ To prepare the filling, beat together the eggs, cheese, garlic, parsley, and black pepper in a large bowl. Set aside.

✳ Pour the water into the pressure cooker. Add the salt and stir to mix. Add the bay leaf. Carefully open up the artichoke leaves slightly, starting from the center and working outward, taking care not to break the leaves. Place the prepared artichokes in the pressure cooker standing up. Drizzle an equal amount of the egg mixture over the artichokes, being certain to spoon some into the center. Drizzle with olive oil.

✳ Position the pressure cooker lid and lock into place. Place over high heat and bring to high pressure. Adjust the heat to stabilize the pressure and cook 7 minutes. Remove from heat and lower pressure using the cold-water release method. Open the pressure cooker. Carefully remove the artichokes using a slotted spoon and place in individual serving bowls. Spoon a couple of tablespoons of the cooking liquid over each artichoke before serving.

NOTE: **The Cold-Water Release Method.** When using a pressure cooker, you will most often want to release the pressure and stop the cooking process as quickly as possible. The best way to do this is to carefully place pressure cooker in sink and run cold water over the lid. You will normally hear a decompressing sound—almost like a swooshing "pop"— once all the pressure has been released.

SERVES 4

ITALIANS LOVE TO stuff THEIR VEGETABLES. THIS IS AN **impressive** FIRST COURSE, MADE EASY BY THE PRESSURE COOKER.

SERVES 6 TO 8

A GREEK SHEEP'S MILK CHEESE, kefalotiri HAS SIMILARITIES TO ITALIAN ROMANO, THOUGH SLIGHTLY LESS SALTY AND LESS ROCK HARD. IT CAN OFTEN BE FOUND IN specialty CHEESE SHOPS AND ETHNIC MARKETS THAT CARRY foods FROM THE MEDITERRANEAN.

Eggplant Stuffed with Onions and Kefalotiri

DIANE KOCHILAS / REPRINTED FROM *THE GREEK VEGETARIAN* (ST. MARTIN'S PRESS)

8 medium-size eggplants (about 1/2 pound each)
1/2 cup olive oil
Salt and freshly ground black pepper
8 small onions, peeled and coarsely chopped (about 6 cups)
4 to 6 cloves garlic, chopped
3 large ripe tomatoes (about 2 pounds) cored, peeled, and coarsely chopped
1 cup coarsely chopped fresh parsley
1/2 pound Greek kefalotiri cut into 1-inch cubes, plus 1/2 cup grated

✴ Leaving the stems on the eggplants, and using a small paring knife, hold each eggplant horizontally and cut through the skin, scooping away about one-third of its flesh from the center. Discard the flesh, or reserve for some other use. Heat 4 to 6 tablespoons of the olive oil in a large skillet and sauté the eggplant until lightly browned and wrinkled. Remove from skillet and place in a lightly oiled baking pan and season with salt and pepper.

✴ Wipe skillet dry. Heat 2 to 3 more tablespoons of olive oil in the skillet and cook the onions for 5 to 6 minutes, until they just start to become transparent. Add the garlic and tomatoes, season with salt and pepper to taste, and simmer, uncovered, for 5 to 8 minutes. Remove from heat, toss in the parsley, and cool slightly. Preheat the oven to 375°F.

✴ Place about 4 cubes of cheese in the belly of each eggplant and fill each eggplant generously with the onions and tomatoes so that they form a mound over the opening. Sprinkle with a little grated cheese. Bake for about 25 minutes, or until eggplants are tender and the cheese is melted. Serve warm.

Baked Dumplings, Roman Style

JAMES MCNAIR / REPRINTED FROM *JAMES MCNAIR COOKS ITALIAN* (CHRONICLE BOOKS)

5 cups milk

1 1/2 teaspoons salt, or to taste

1/2 teaspoon freshly ground black pepper, or to taste

1/8 teaspoon freshly grated nutmeg, or to taste

1 1/2 cups coarsely ground semolina flour, preferably imported from Italy

1/2 cup freshly grated Parmesan cheese, preferably Parmigiano-Reggiano

3 egg yolks, lightly beaten

3 tablespoons minced fresh sage, or 1 tablespoon crumbled dried sage

2 tablespoons unsalted butter, melted

Softened unsalted butter for greasing baking sheet and dish and for dotting on top

✹ In a large, heavy-bottomed saucepan, combine the milk, salt, pepper, and nutmeg over medium heat. Bring the milk almost to a boil. Reduce the heat to the lowest possible setting, and gradually pour in the semolina in a thin, steady stream, stirring constantly with a wooden spoon or a wire whisk. The mixture will thicken quickly, but continue cooking and stirring, scraping the bottom of the pan, until the mixture forms a very thick mass that pulls away from the sides of the pan, about 15 minutes. Remove from heat.

✹ Quickly stir ¼ cup of the Parmesan cheese, the egg yolks, sage, and the melted butter into the hot semolina mixture, stirring well.

✹ Grease a large, shallow baking sheet with softened butter. Using a metal spatula dipped in cold water from time to time, spread the thick mixture into a layer about ¼ inch thick. Let cool to room temperature, then cover and refrigerate until the mixture is cold and firm, about 1 hour.

✹ Preheat oven to 400°F. Grease a 9 x 13-inch baking dish with softened butter and set aside.

✹ Using a biscuit cutter or straight-sided glass about 1½ to 2 inches in diameter, cut the semolina sheet into rounds, dipping the cutter into cold water between cuts. Place the dumplings in the prepared baking dish, arranging them in slightly overlapping rows to form a single layer. Dot with softened butter and sprinkle the remaining ¼ cup Parmesan cheese.

✹ Place in the preheated oven and bake until golden and crusty, about 20 minutes. Remove from oven and let stand about 5 minutes before serving directly from the baking dish.

SERVES 6 TO 8

UNLIKE most ITALIAN FIRST COURSES, THIS DISH CAN BE PREPARED A DAY OR TWO IN advance AND REFRIGERATED, THEN baked AT THE LAST MINUTE. SEMOLINA IS GROUND FROM HARD DURUM WHEAT; LOOK FOR IT IN specialty FOOD STORES, ITALIAN markets, AND SOME SUPERMARKETS.

Pacific Rim Risotto

3 cloves garlic
1 medium onion, quartered
1 tablespoon fresh ginger, peeled and minced
2 tablespoons olive oil
4 large boneless, skinless chicken breasts (about 1 pound total), each breast cut into 4 diagonal pieces
1 cup uncooked arborio rice
2 cups quartered white mushrooms, such as crimini

2 to 3 cups unsalted chicken broth
1/4 cup dry white wine or sherry
1 tablespoon sesame oil
1 teaspoon hot chile sauce
1/2 pound smoked linguisa (Portuguese) sausage (or other hot, smoked sausage), cut into 1 1/2-inch diagonal pieces
1/2 cup freshly grated Parmesan cheese
1/2 cup roasted cashews
1 cup unpacked cilantro leaves, for garnish

✳ In a food processor, finely chop garlic, onion, and ginger. Set aside.

✳ In a deep, large, heavy-bottomed skillet with a cover, heat olive oil. Add chicken breast pieces and cook over medium-high heat, until lightly golden and plump, about 3 minutes per side. Remove chicken from pan. Add onion mixture to skillet and sauté until translucent, 4 to 5 minutes.

✳ Add rice to pan and continue to sauté for 1 minute longer. Add mushrooms, 2 cups of the stock, sherry or wine, sesame oil, and chile sauce. Bring to a low simmer, cover, and simmer for 15 minutes (add more stock if mixture appears dry at this point).

✳ Gently place sausage pieces and chicken on top of rice mixture (do not mix in). Cover and continue to cook over medium heat for another 10 minutes.

✳ Fold in cheese and place on serving platter or shallow bowl. Sprinkle with cashews and cilantro. Serve immediately.

SERVES 6

CHUNKY bites OF CHICKEN AND SAUSAGE COMBINED WITH THE creamy RISOTTO MAKE THIS A COMPLETE MEAL WHEN SERVED WITH A simple GREEN SALAD.

Eggplant and Tomato Hobo Pack with Lemon and Garlic

CHRIS SCHLESINGER AND JOHN WILLOUGHBY/ REPRINTED FROM *LICENSE TO GRILL* (WILLIAM MORROW AND COMPANY)

SERVES 4 TO 6

IN THIS DISH, THE LEMONS soften, TURN A LITTLE BROWN, AND GIVE OFF SOME AROMATIC flavor, AS WELL AS ACTING AS A HEAT SHIELD OF SORTS FOR THE OTHER INGREDIENTS.

2 lemons, sliced into thin rounds
2 small eggplants, cut lengthwise into quarters
4 plum tomatoes, halved

2 heads garlic, halved horizontally
7 large sprigs fresh oregano or rosemary
1/4 cup olive oil
Salt and freshly ground black pepper

✳ Start fire.

✳ Lay out 2 sheets of heavy-duty aluminum foil, each about 2 feet long, one on top of the other. Place the lemon slices into the center, then put the eggplant quarters on top. Follow with the tomatoes and garlic, add the herbs, and drizzle with the olive oil. Season with salt and pepper to taste. Lay a third length of heavy-duty foil over the top. Fold the edges of the sheets together on all sides, closing the pack, then roll them up until they bump into the food, forming a ridge around its perimeter. Place the pack right side up in the center of a fourth length of foil and fold the four sides over the top of the packet, one after another.

✳ The package is now ready for the coals. The fire should have passed its peak of intensity and be dying down, so that it consists primarily of glowing coals covered with a thin film of ash, but very few flickering flames. Clear a place for the foil packet, leaving a thin layer of coals upon which to place the packet. Place the packet on the cleared area and heap up coals all around, but not directly on top. Cook, keeping watch and shifting the packet as needed so it is in continuous contact with the glowing coals, for 20 to 30 minutes, depending upon the intensity of the coals.

✳ Remove from the coals, unroll the foil, and serve at once.

Orange–Sweet Potato Hobo Pack

CHRIS SCHLESINGER AND JOHN WILLOUGHBY/ REPRINTED FROM *LICENSE TO GRILL*
(WILLIAM MORROW AND COMPANY)

4 medium sweet potatoes, washed but not peeled, cut into rounds about 2 inches thick
1 orange, thinly sliced (including peel)
1 large red onion, peeled and quartered
1/3 cup raisins
1/4 cup olive oil

1/4 cup unsalted butter, cut into small bits
Salt and freshly ground black pepper to taste
1/3 cup fresh lemon juice (about 1 large lemon)
1/3 cup honey
1/3 cup roughly chopped parsley

✳ In a large bowl, combine the sweet potatoes, orange, onion, raisins, olive oil, and butter. Toss lightly, sprinkle with salt and pepper to taste, and toss lightly again.

✳ Start fire.

✳ Lay out 2 sheets of heavy-duty foil, each about 2 feet long, one on top of the other. Place the sweet potato mixture in the center, then lay a third length of heavy-duty foil over the top. Fold the edges of the sheets together on all sides, closing the pack, continuing to roll until sides come up against the food, forming a ridge around its perimeter. Place the pack right side up in the center of a fourth length of foil and fold the four sides over the top of the packet.

✳ The package is now ready for the coals. The fire should have passed its peak of intensity and be dying down, so that it consists primarily of glowing coals covered with a thin film of gray ash but very few flickering flames. Clear a place in the coals for the packet, leaving a thin layer of coals. Place the packet on the cleared area and heap up coals all around, but not directly on top. Cook, keeping watch and shifting the packet as needed, so it is continuously in contact with glowing coals, for 30 to 35 minutes, depending upon the intensity of the coals.

✳ While the hobo pack is cooking, combine the lemon juice, honey, and parsley in a small bowl and mix well to combine.

✳ Remove foil packet from the coals, unroll foil, drizzle the vegetables with the lemon-honey mixture, and serve at once.

SERVES 4

Grillmaster CHRIS SCHLESINGER USES THE HEAT OF THE coals TO MAKE A FIRE-ROASTED version OF CANDIED SWEET POTATOES. YOU CAN'T BEAT THIS DISH FOR AN autumn OR WINTER DINNER.

Pasta Shells Stuffed with Gorgonzola and Hazelnuts

One 12-ounce box jumbo pasta shells

Stuffing
One tablespoon olive oil
6 cloves garlic, minced
One 10-ounce box frozen spinach, defrosted and gently squeezed of excess water
1 pound part-skim ricotta cheese
1/4 pound gorgonzola cheese

1 pound part-skim grated mozzarella
1 teaspoon salt
1/2 teaspoon freshly ground black pepper
1 egg
2 tablespoons milk
4 ounces hazelnuts (walnuts can be substituted)

One 26-ounce jar tomato sauce
1 cup grated Parmesan cheese

SERVES 4

HERE'S A great ONE-DISH meal. WALNUTS CAN BE SUBSTITUTED FOR THE HAZELNUTS.

✳ Cook pasta in boiling water according to directions on package. Rinse under cold water and drain well. Set aside.

✳ In a medium-size sauté pan, warm oil. Add garlic and cook over a low heat for about 2 minutes. Add spinach and sauté until all excess moisture is cooked out, about 3 to 5 minutes. Place spinach in a large mixing bowl.

✳ Add ricotta, gorgonzola, and half of the mozzarella to spinach in bowl and combine well. Add salt, pepper, egg, and milk and blend all ingredients.

✳ Preheat oven to 350°F. Place nuts on a baking sheet and roast 6 to 8 minutes, shaking pan occasionally, until fragrant. Remove from baking sheet and allow to cool on plate. When cool, roughly chop by hand or in a food processor. Set aside.

✳ Coat a 9 x 13-inch pan with vegetable oil spray. Thinly coat the bottom of the pan with 2 to 3 cups of the tomato sauce, depending upon how saucy you want final dish to be.

✳ With a soup spoon, fill pasta shells with spinach and cheese stuffing. As shells are filled, place in prepared pan, open side up. Top with remaining mozzarella and the Parmesan cheese. Sprinkle with chopped nuts. Bake for 40 to 45 minutes, until bubbly and golden.

Savory Bread Pudding Layered with Asparagus, Fontina, and Mixed Spring Herbs

GEORGEANNE BRENNAN / REPRINTED FROM *POTAGER* (CHRONICLE BOOKS)

12 to 16 thick slices of dry bread	¼ cup freshly grated Romano cheese
2½ to 3 cups milk	4 ounces fontina cheese, slivered
1 pound asparagus	4 ounces Swiss cheese, slivered
3 eggs	½ cup chopped fresh herbs, such as chives,
1 teaspoon salt	parsley, tarragon, sage, or thyme
1 teaspoon freshly ground black pepper	1 tablespoon butter, cut into small pieces

✻ Place the bread in a single layer in a shallow baking dish. Pour 2½ cups of the milk over the top. Let soak until the bread has absorbed the milk and becomes soft, about 30 minutes. Press the bread slices to extract the milk. Measure the milk; you should have ½ cup milk left after squeezing the bread. If not, make up the difference with the additional ½ cup milk as needed. Set the milk and bread aside.

✻ While the bread is soaking, trim the asparagus, removing the woody ends. Cut the stalks on the diagonal into thin slivers each about 2 inches long and ⅜ inch thick. Arrange the slivered asparagus on a steamer rack and place over gently boiling water. Cover and steam until barely tender, 2 to 3 minutes. Immediately place the asparagus under cold running water until cold. Drain and set aside.

✻ Preheat the oven to 350°F. Butter a 3-quart mold. (A soufflé dish works well.)

✻ In a medium bowl beat together the eggs, salt, pepper, and the ½ cup milk until well blended. Layer one-third of the bread in the prepared dish. Set 6 to 8 asparagus slivers aside and top the bread layer with half of the remaining asparagus and half of the mixed herbs. Strew one-third of each of the cheeses over the asparagus. Repeat the layers, using half of the remaining bread, all of the remaining asparagus and herbs, and half of the remaining cheese. Arrange the remaining bread on top, strew the remaining cheese over it, and garnish with the reserved asparagus slivers. Pour the egg mixture over the layers and then dot with butter.

✻ Bake in the preheated oven until the top is crusty brown and a knife inserted in the middle of the pudding comes out clean, about 45 minutes.

Yogurt Sauce

MICHEL ROUX / REPRINTED FROM *SAUCES* (RIZZOLI)

2¹/₂ cups plain yogurt
¹/₂ cup mayonnaise
2 tablespoons snipped fresh herbs of your choice (such as chervil, parsley, chives, or tarragon)

1 medium tomato, peeled, seeded, and diced
Small pinch of cayenne (4 drops of hot pepper sauce can be substituted)
Salt to taste

✴ Mix all ingredients together. Sauce can be served at room temperature or chilled.

SERVES 8

THIS refreshing SAUCE IS EXCELLENT WITH all COLD VEGETABLES, COLD PASTA, FISH, and HARD-BOILED EGGS.

Bois Boudran Sauce

MICHEL ROUX / REPRINTED FROM *SAUCES* (RIZZOLI)

²/₃ cup peanut oil
3¹/₂ tablespoons red wine vinegar
Salt and freshly ground black pepper
5 tablespoons ketchup
1 teaspoon Worcestershire sauce

5 drops hot pepper sauce
²/₃ cup chopped shallots
2 tablespoons finely snipped chervil
2 tablespoons finely snipped chives
¹/₂ cup finely snipped tarragon

✴ In a medium bowl, combine the oil, vinegar, a pinch of salt, and three turns of a pepper mill. Stir with a small whisk, then whisk in the ketchup, Worcestershire sauce, pepper sauce, shallots, and all the snipped herbs. Adjust seasonings with salt and pepper and keep sauce at room temperature. (The sauce is ready to use right away, but it can also be kept in an airtight container in the refrigerator for 3 days.)

SERVES 6

AN excellent SAUCE FOR GRILLED OR ROASTED CHICKEN OR POUSSIN, BOIS BOUDRAN sauce CAN ALSO BE USED TO COAT SALMON OR LIGHTLY poached TROUT JUST BEFORE SERVING.

MAIN DISHES

Peppered Beef with Flat Rice Noodles

STEVEN WONG / REPRINTED FROM *NEW WORLD NOODLES* **(ROBERT ROSE)**

Marinade
1 tablespoon oyster sauce
1 tablespoon soy sauce
1 teaspoon coarsely ground black pepper
2 tablespoons dry sherry
1 1/2 teaspoons cornstarch
3/4 pound sirloin steak, cut into thin strips

Sauce
1 tablespoon soy sauce
1/4 cup chicken stock

1 pound fresh, flat rice noodles or fresh fettuccine
2 tablespoons vegetable oil
3 tablespoons finely chopped shallots
1 tablespoon finely chopped fresh ginger
1 tablespoon finely chopped garlic
3/4 cup thinly sliced green bell pepper
3/4 cup thinly sliced red pepper
1 cup bean sprouts, packed
Freshly ground black pepper

SERVES 4

IN this CHINESE VERSION OF PEPPER STEAK, THE peppers CAN BE REPLACED WITH CABBAGE OR BROCCOLI.

✱ In a medium bowl, combine all of the marinade ingredients. Add beef strips and marinate for 20 minutes.

✱ In a small bowl, prepare sauce by combining soy sauce and chicken stock. Set aside.

✱ If using fresh rice noodles, break them up by placing in a colander, running hot water over them and separating the strands with your fingers. If using fettuccine, prepare according to package directions, drain, and coat with a little oil.

✱ In a nonstick wok or skillet, heat oil over high heat for 30 seconds. Add shallots, ginger, and garlic and stir-fry for 30 seconds. Add beef and marinade and stir-fry for 2 minutes, stirring to separate pieces. Add peppers and stir-fry 2 minutes longer. Add noodles and sauce, stirring constantly until heated through. Add bean sprouts and mix well. Season to taste with freshly ground pepper and serve immediately.

Grilled Steak with Spicy Guajillo Sauce

RICK BAYLESS / REPRINTED FROM *RICK BAYLESS'S MEXICAN KITCHEN* (SCRIBNER)

SERVES 6

SMOKY, CHARCOALED BEEF LIT UP BY THE slow-simmered GUAJILLO SAUCE IS ONE OF THE CROWNING glories OF THE MEXICAN KITCHEN. THE SAUCE CAN BE MADE SEVERAL DAYS IN ADVANCE AND THE steaks CAN BE SLIPPED INTO THE MARINADE UP TO 4 HOURS BEFORE grilling.

Guajillo Sauce

6 cloves garlic, unpeeled

16 guajillo chilies, stemmed and seeded (about 4 ounces total)

1 teaspoon dried oregano, preferably Mexican

1/4 teaspoon black pepper, preferably freshly ground

1/8 teaspoon cumin, preferably freshly ground

3 2/3 cups beef broth, plus a little more if needed

2 1/2 tablespoons vegetable or olive oil

Salt, about 1 1/2 teaspoons, depending on the saltiness of the broth

Sugar, about 1 1/2 teaspoons

1 tablespoon cider vinegar

Six 6-ounce beef steaks, such as tenderloin, New York strip, or sirloin, about 1 inch thick

1 large red onion, cut into 1/2-inch-thick slices

Several sprigs of cilantro, for garnish

✱ To make guajillo sauce, roast the unpeeled garlic cloves directly on an ungreased griddle or heavy skillet over medium heat, turning occasionally, until soft (they'll blacken in spots), about 15 minutes; cool and peel.

✱ While the garlic is roasting, toast the chilies on another side of the griddle or skillet, 1 or 2 at a time, opening them flat and pressing them down hard onto the hot cooking surface with a spatula. When chilies crackle, or even send up a wisp of smoke, flip and press down hard on other side with spatula.

✱ Place cooked chilies in a small bowl with hot water and let rehydrate for 30 minutes, stirring frequently to ensure even soaking. Drain and discard the water.

✱ Combine the oregano, black pepper, and cumin in a food processor or blender, along with the garlic, drained chilies, and 2/3 cup of the broth. Blend to a smooth purée, scraping and stirring every few seconds. (If the mixture won't go through the blender blades, add a little more liquid.) Press through a medium-mesh sieve into a bowl.

✱ Heat 1 1/2 tablespoons of the oil in a heavy, medium-size pot (such as a Dutch oven or Mexican *cazuela*) over medium-high heat. When the oil is hot enough to make a drop of the purée sizzle sharply, add the purée and stir constantly until it reduces to a thick paste, 5 to 7 minutes. Stir in the remaining 3 cups of broth, partially cover, and simmer over a medium-low heat, stirring occasionally, for about 45 minutes, for the flavors to come together. If necessary, stir in a little broth to bring mixture to a medium, saucy consistency. Taste and season with about 1 teaspoon of the salt and the sugar.

✱ To marinate the steaks, mix ¼ cup of the sauce with the vinegar and the remaining ½ teaspoon of salt in a large bowl. Lay the steaks in marinade and turn to coat evenly. Let marinate, covered and refrigerated, while preparing the fire. (It is best not to let the steaks marinate for longer than 4 hours, because it will affect the color and texture of the meat.)

✱ Light a gas grill or prepare a charcoal fire, letting the coals burn until they are covered with gray ash and are medium-hot. Position the grill grate about 8 inches above the coals and lightly oil. Lay the steaks on the hottest portion of the grill and let them sear for 4 to 5 minutes on one side, then turn and finish on the other (4 to 5 minutes more for medium-rare).

✱ While the steaks are cooking, separate the onion into rings and toss them with the remaining 1 tablespoon of oil. Spread them on the grill around the steaks and cook, stirring and turning with tongs or a spatula, until lightly browned and crisp-tender, 6 to 8 minutes.

✱ As the steaks and onion are done, heat the sauce to a simmer. Serve steaks as soon as they come off the grill with a generous serving of the sauce and a topping of the onions. Garnish with sprigs of cilantro.

VARIATIONS: Anything tender enough to be grillable can be used in this dish, from beef steaks, to pork chops and tenderloin, to chicken, duck, and quail, to shrimp, scallops, and fish steaks, to vegetables like sweet potato, zucchini, and eggplant.

Beef Daube with Dried Cèpes

GEORGEANNE BRENNAN / REPRINTED FROM *THE FOOD AND FLAVORS OF HAUTE PROVENCE* **(CHRONICLE BOOKS)**

4 pounds boneless beef chuck roast or
   a combination of boneless chuck and
   beef shank
2 yellow onions
3 carrots
8 fresh thyme branches, each about
   6 inches long
2 bay leaves
1 fresh rosemary branch, about 6 inches
   long
2 teaspoons salt
2 tablespoons freshly ground black pepper
4 cloves garlic

1 orange zest strip, 4 inches long and
   1/2 inch wide
1 bottle (750 ml) dry red wine such as
   Côtes du Rhône, Zinfandel, or Burgundy
1/3 cup minced roulade (peppered
   pancetta) or salt pork
2 tablespoons all-purpose flour
1 cup water
2 ounces dried cèpes, some broken into
   2 or 3 pieces, others left whole
1 pound wide, flat dried pasta noodles
1/2 to 3/4 cup grated Parmesan cheese
1/2 cup chopped fresh flat-leaf parsley

❋ Cut the beef chuck into 2- to 2½-inch squares. Trim off and discard any large pieces of fat. If using beef shank, cut the meat from the bone in pieces as large as possible. Place the meat in a large enamel, glass, earthenware, or other nonreactive bowl.

❋ Quarter one of the onions, and add the pieces to the meat along with the carrots, thyme, bay leaves, rosemary, one teaspoon of salt, one tablespoon of the pepper, 2 cloves of the garlic, and the orange zest. Pour the wine over all and turn to mix and immerse the ingredients. Cover and marinate in the refrigerator for at least 4 hours, or as long as overnight.

❋ To cook the daube, put the roulade or salt pork in a heavy-bottomed casserole or a Dutch oven large enough to hold the marinating mixture. Place over medium-low heat and cook, stirring occasionally until the fat is released, about 5 minutes. Discard the crisped bits of roulade or salt pork.

❋ Dice the remaining onion and mince the remaining 2 garlic cloves, and add to the fat. Sauté over medium heat until translucent, 3 to 5 minutes. Remove with a slotted spoon and set aside.

❋ Drain the meat and reserve the marinade. Pat the meat as dry as possible. Do not be concerned by the meat's purplish color, as this is caused by the wine. Add the meat to the pot a few pieces at a time and sauté for about 5 minutes, turning them once or twice. The meat will darken in color, but will not truly "brown."

(continued on next page)

SERVES 6 TO 8

DAUBES REQUIRE THE LESS tender CUTS OF BEEF, WHICH HAVE GELATINOUS SINEWS AND TENDONS THAT thicken AND flavor THE SAUCE. GEORGEANNE BRENNAN STARTS THIS AT LEAST A DAY IN ADVANCE, SO THAT THE MEAT CAN marinate OVERNIGHT. THE MEAT IS SIMMERED THE NEXT DAY, AND CAN EASILY WAIT, ITS FLAVORS EVER DEEPENING, FOR THE DAY after IT IS COOKED TO BE SERVED.

DRIED cèpes ARE MORE LIKELY TO BE LABELED UNDER THEIR ITALIAN NAME, *porcini*, IN THE UNITED STATES.

✳ Remove the pieces with a slotted spoon and continue cooking until all the meat has been sautéed. When the last of the meat pieces has been removed, add the flour and cook until it browns, stirring often.

✳ Raise the heat to high and slowly pour in the reserved marinade and all of its ingredients. Deglaze the pan by scraping up any bits clinging to the bottom. Return the sautéed onion, garlic, meat, and any collected juices to the pan. Add the remaining teaspoon of salt and the remaining tablespoon of pepper, the water, and the mushrooms and bring to a boil. Reduce the heat to very low, cover with a tight-fitting lid, and simmer until the meat can be cut through with the edge of a spoon and the liquid has thickened, 2½ to 3 hours.

✳ Remove daube from heat. Discard the carrots, herb branches, and onion quarters. Skim off some, but not all, of the fat, as some is necessary to coat the pasta.

✳ Meanwhile, bring a large pot of salted water to a boil. Add the pasta, stir well, and cook until just tender. Drain.

✳ Put the pasta in a warmed serving bowl and ladle some of the sauce from the daube over it, adding more salt and pepper, if desired, and topping with ¼ cup of the Parmesan cheese and the parsley. Serve the daube directly from its cooking vessel, or from a serving bowl. Pass remaining cheese at the table.

Chicken Cordon Bleu Meatloaf

PETER KAUFMAN AND T.K. WOODS / REPRINTED FROM *THE GREAT AMERICAN MEATLOAF CONTEST COOKBOOK* **(WILLIAM MORROW AND COMPANY)**

Loaf

1 1/2 pounds ground chicken
2 large eggs, lightly beaten
1 cup fresh bread crumbs (more may be
   needed to make a firm loaf)
2 tablespoons milk or half-and-half
1 tablespoon chopped fresh parsley
1 teaspoon salt
1/2 teaspoon black pepper
1/2 teaspoon ground allspice

Filling

4 slices low-fat turkey ham
4 slices low-fat Swiss cheese

Mushroom Sauce

4 tablespoons butter or margarine
1 cup sliced mushrooms
1 tablespoon minced shallots
1 chicken bouillon cube
1/2 cup dry white wine
1 tablespoon cornstarch
1 cup heavy cream or half-and-half

✱ Preheat the oven to 375°F. Lightly coat a 9 x 5 x 3-inch loaf pan with nonstick cooking spray.

✱ In a large bowl, mix all of the loaf ingredients.

✱ Put the loaf mixture on a lightly oiled piece of aluminum foil resting on a cookie sheet, and press the mixture into a 7 x 10-inch rectangle. Place the ham and cheese slices on the rectangle. Cover with another piece of aluminum foil and refrigerate for 1 hour until firm.

✱ Roll up the loaf, starting at the smaller side, using the foil to lift and nudge the mixture into shape. Seal the edges and ends of the loaf.

✱ Place rolled loaf in prepared pan. Bake for 1 hour, or until the top is brown and sides pull away.

✱ In a medium-size skillet, melt the butter over medium heat. Cook the mushrooms and shallots until soft, about 3 minutes. Add the bouillon cube and wine.

✱ In a small bowl, mix the cornstarch and cream, or half-and-half, until smooth. Add to the mushroom mixture and cook until thickened.

✱ Let the loaf sit for 10 minutes before slicing. Serve with mushroom sauce.

SERVES 6 TO 8

THIS appetizing MEATLOAF WON THE FIRST PLACE prize IN THE POULTRY CATEGORY OF THE 1992 GREAT AMERICAN meatloaf NATIONAL RECIPE CONTEST. A FOOD PROCESSOR IS perfect FOR GRINDING ANY BONE-LESS CHICKEN MEAT.

Popeye Meatloaf

PETER KAUFMAN AND T. K. WOODS / REPRINTED FROM *THE GREAT AMERICAN MEATLOAF CONTEST COOKBOOK* **(WILLIAM MORROW AND COMPANY)**

SERVES 8 TO 10

MAGGI IS A FLAVORFUL, ORGANIC seasoning MIX, USUALLY AVAILABLE IN THE DRY soup SECTION OF YOUR SUPERMARKET. IF UNAVAILABLE, SUBSTITUTE 2 teaspoons OF YOUR FAVORITE SEASONING MIX.

One 10-ounce package frozen spinach
3 pounds ground beef
1 pound Italian sausage, casing removed
1/2 cup plain bread crumbs (more may be necessary to make a firm loaf)
1/2 cup freshly grated Parmesan or Romano cheese
1 tablespoon butter

2 tablespoons olive oil
1 cup diced onions
2 garlic cloves, minced
4 large eggs, lightly beaten
2 teaspoons Maggi
1/8 teaspoon salt
1/8 teaspoon black pepper
2 strips uncooked bacon

✱ Preheat the oven to 350°F. Lightly oil a 10 x 13-inch roasting pan.

✱ Thaw the frozen spinach and squeeze out the excess moisture. Coarsely chop the spinach leaves.

✱ In a large bowl, place the ground beef, sausage, bread crumbs, grated cheese, and chopped spinach leaves. Mix and set aside.

✱ In a skillet, melt the butter with the olive oil and sauté the onion and garlic until translucent, about 4 to 6 minutes. When cool, add the sautéed ingredients to the meatloaf mixture.

✱ In a small bowl, combine the eggs, Maggi, salt, and pepper. Add this to the meat mixture. Mix well.

✱ Shape the meat mixture into a loaf and place it in the prepared pan. Lay the bacon strips across the top of the meatloaf. Bake for 45 minutes to 1 hour, or until done.

New California Patty Melts

JAMES MCNAIR / REPRINTED FROM *JAMES MCNAIR'S BURGERS* (CHRONICLE BOOKS)

3 tablespoons unsalted butter
2 cups thinly sliced yellow onion
1 pound ground beef
2 teaspoons Worcestershire sauce, or
    to taste

Salt and freshly ground black pepper
8 rye bread slices
4 ounces creamy goat's milk cheese
Vegetable oil for brushing on grill rack
Variety of mustards for serving

✳ In a medium-size sauté pan or skillet, melt the butter over medium heat. Add the onion, cover, reduce the heat to low, and cook, stirring from time to time, for 15 minutes. Remove cover, and continue to cook the onion over low heat until very soft and golden, about 45 minutes longer, stirring to keep onions from sticking to pan.

✳ In a grill, prepare a hot fire for direct heat cooking or preheat a broiler.

✳ While onions are cooking and after fire has been lit, combine ground beef, Worcestershire sauce, and salt and pepper to taste in a large bowl. Handling the meat as little as possible to avoid compacting it, mix ingredients together well. Divide the mixture into 8 equal portions and form into thin, round patties to fit the bread slices. Cut the cheese into 4 pieces a little smaller than the patties. Place a piece of cheese on 4 of the patties, cover with the remaining patties, and press edges together to seal and encase the cheese.

✳ When the fire is ready, brush the grill rack or broiler rack with vegetable oil. Place the patties on the grill rack or under the broiler and cook until browned, about 4 minutes. With a wide spatula, turn the patties and cook until done to preference, about 4 minutes longer for medium-rare. During the last few minutes of cooking, place the bread slices on the outer edges of the grill to toast lightly or prepare in toaster.

✳ Top 4 slices of the bread with the patties, pile on the onion, and cover with the remaining bread slices. Offer mustards at the table.

SERVES 4

CHÈVRE AND CARAMELIZED ONIONS add AN UPDATED TASTE TO THIS LOS ANGELES classic, USUALLY MADE WITH CHEDDAR CHEESE AND grilled ONION.

Lamb Burgers and Potato Petals

SERVES 6

GRILLING THE POTATOES
MAKES THEM light AND
CRISPY, WHILE THE YOGURT
AND mint PROVIDE A RE-
FRESHING GREEK-INSPIRED
zip TO THE BURGERS.

Yogurt Sauce
1¹/₂ cups nonfat yogurt or a combination
    of nonfat yogurt and low-fat sour cream
¹/₂ teaspoon salt

Potato Petals
2¹/₂ pounds potatoes (Yukon Golds, Idaho,
    or baking potatoes)
1 tablespoon olive oil
1 teaspoon each: dried thyme, oregano,
    marjoram, salt and pepper, or to taste

Lamb Burgers
4 cloves garlic, peeled
1 medium onion, peeled and roughly
    chopped

1 tablespoon olive oil
1 teaspoon each: ground cumin, ground
    coriander, red pepper flakes, salt and
    pepper, or to taste
1 pound chopped fresh spinach or one
    10-ounce box frozen spinach, thawed
    and squeezed
1 cup unpacked fresh mint leaves, or
    2 tablespoons dried mint
1¹/₂ cups unpacked fresh flat-leaf parsley
    (reserve ¹/₂ cup for garnish)
1¹/₂ pounds ground lamb (if using patties,
    make sure they are not preseasoned)

✱ To make yogurt sauce, mix together yogurt and salt. Set aside in refrigerator.

✱ To make potato petals, slice potatoes on diagonal bias into ¹/₃-inch slices. Lay in a single layer on a baking sheet. Sprinkle and toss with olive oil, herbs, salt and pepper. Set aside.

✱ Start fire.

✱ To make burgers, place garlic and onion in a food processor fitted with a metal blade. Pulse until finely chopped.

✱ In a large sauté pan over medium-high heat, warm olive oil. Add garlic and onions, and sauté until translucent, about 3 minutes. Add spices and continue to sauté, stirring often, for another minute (be careful not to burn spices).

✱ Add chopped spinach, mint, and parsley to onion mixture. Stir well, cover, and allow spinach to wilt, about 3 to 5 minutes. Place mixture in a large mixing bowl.

✱ Add ground lamb to onion-spinach mixture and gently mix ingredients together. Form into 6 patties.

✱ Place potatoes on grill and grill for about 7 to 8 minutes per side, until puffed and golden brown. Add patties to grill and cook for about 4 to 5 minutes per side.

✱ To assemble the dish, fan potato slices onto serving plate. Place a burger at the base of potato fan. Drizzle yogurt sauce over entire plate and garnish with reserved parsley. Serve immediately.

Three Nut Turkey Burger

JAMES MCNAIR / REPRINTED FROM *JAMES MCNAIR'S BURGERS* (CHRONICLE BOOKS)

Tropical Fruit Salsa
1 star fruit (carambola)
1 small, ripe mango, peeled, pitted, and
    cut into 1/4-inch dice
1/2 cup red seedless grapes, coarsely
    chopped
1 banana, peeled and cut into 1/2-inch dice
1/3 small cantaloupe, peeled, seeded, and
    cut into 1/4-inch dice
1/2 cup diced (1/4-inch) pineapple, fresh or
    canned in its own juices
1 fresh jalapeño pepper, stemmed and cut
    into very small squares

Grated zest and juice of 1 lime
1/4 cup freshly squeezed orange juice

Turkey Burgers
1/2 cup (about 2 ounces) filberts
1/2 cup (about 2 ounces) almonds
1/2 cup (about 1 1/2 ounces) walnuts
1 tablespoon peanut oil
2 cups shredded Monterey Jack cheese
1 pound lean ground turkey
4 whole-wheat hamburger buns, split
Vegetable oil for brushing on grill rack
Red leaf lettuce leaves

SERVES 4

THEODORE SKIBA FROM

TEQUESTA, FLORIDA, WAS

awarded THE JUDGE'S

AWARD FOR CREATIVITY

FOR THIS zesty ENTRY

IN THE BUILD-A-BETTER-

burger CONTEST.

✱ To make the salsa, cut half of the star fruit into 1/4-inch dice. Slice the remaining star fruit crosswise and reserve for garnish. In a large bowl, combine the remaining salsa ingredients. Stir well to blend, cover, and refrigerate for at least 1 hour or up to 3 hours.

✱ To make the burgers, chop 5 tablespoons of each type of nut. Heat the peanut oil in a medium-size nonstick skillet over medium-high heat. Add the chopped nuts and sauté until lightly toasted, about 5 minutes. Combine the toasted nuts with 1 cup of the cheese and set aside. Grind the remaining nuts together in a food processor and set aside.

✱ Divide the ground turkey into 8 equal portions and form into patties to fit buns. Distribute nut and cheese mixture evenly over the tops of the patties. Cover with the remaining patties and press the edges together to seal. Spread the remaining ground nut mixture on a large, flat plate and press both sides of each burger into the nuts, pressing hard enough for good adhesion.

✱ In a grill with a cover, prepare a hot fire for direct heat cooking.

✱ When the fire is ready, brush the grill rack with vegetable oil. Place the patties on the grill, cover, and cook until browned on the bottom, about 4 minutes. With a wide spatula, turn the patties, replace cover, and cook until juices run clear when the patties are pierced, about 5 minutes longer. During the last few minutes of cooking, distribute the remaining cup of cheese evenly over the tops of the burgers to melt. Place the buns, cut side down, on the outer edge of the grill to lightly toast.

✱ To serve, spoon 2 to 3 tablespoons of the salsa on the bottoms of the buns. Add the patties, top each with about 1 tablespoon of the salsa and a lettuce leaf, and cover with the bun tops. Serve immediately.

Chicken Cutlets with Prosciutto and Sage

JAMES MCNAIR / REPRINTED FROM *JAMES MCNAIR COOKS ITALIAN* **(CHRONICLE BOOKS)**

4 boneless, skinless chicken breast halves
Salt
Freshly ground black pepper
3 ounces thinly sliced prosciutto
8 whole fresh sage leaves

About 4 tablespoons ($1/2$ stick) unsalted butter
About 2 tablespoons olive oil
1 cup dry white wine

✳ Rinse chicken breasts under cold water and pat dry with paper towels. Trim away the tendons and any connective tissue or fat from the breasts. Separate the little fillet from each breast and reserve for another use.

✳ Place each chicken breast between 2 sheets of waxed paper or plastic wrap and pound with mallet or other flat, heavy instrument to a uniform thickness of about $1/8$ inch. Lightly sprinkle the chicken with salt and pepper.

✳ Trim the prosciutto slices to fit precisely on top of chicken breasts. Top each chicken piece with a slice of prosciutto and 1 or 2 sage leaves, securing each leaf in place with a toothpick.

✳ In a heavy-bottomed sauté pan or skillet (without a nonstick coating), combine 2 tablespoons butter and 2 tablespoons olive oil over medium-high heat. When the butter stops foaming, add as many of the chicken pieces as will fit comfortably without crowding the pan. Brown on one side, turn, and cook on the other side until browned and opaque all the way through, 4 to 5 minutes total. Use a small, sharp knife to check doneness. Transfer the chicken to a warmed plate and cover to keep warm. Cook the remaining chicken in the same way, adding a little more butter and oil if necessary to prevent sticking.

✳ When all the chicken is cooked, discard the cooking fat from the pan. Return the pan to medium-high heat. Add the white wine and salt and pepper to taste to the pan and scrape the bottom of the pan with a wooden spoon to loosen any browned bits. Reduce the wine by half, add the remaining 2 tablespoons of butter and stir until melted. Discard the toothpicks and transfer chicken breasts to 4 individual plates. Pour the sauce over the chicken and serve.

Chicken with Yogurt and Beer

TOM LACALAMITA / REPRINTED FROM *THE ULTIMATE PRESSURE COOKER COOKBOOK* **(SIMON & SCHUSTER)**

2 chicken breasts, split (about 2 pounds)
3 tablespoons olive oil
1 large onion, cut in half and thinly sliced
1 cup plain yogurt
1/2 cup beer

1/2 teaspoon paprika
1/2 teaspoon oregano
1 1/2 teaspoons salt
1/8 teaspoon freshly ground black pepper

✳ Remove and discard the skin and any visible fat from the chicken. Cut the breast halves into 3 or 4 small pieces, cutting straight through the bone.

✳ Heat the olive oil in a pressure cooker over high heat. Add the chicken a few pieces at a time and brown evenly on all sides. Remove and set aside on a large plate or platter. Reduce heat to medium, add onion, and sauté for 4 to 5 minutes, or until soft. Stir frequently so that the onion does not brown.

✳ Add chicken back to pressure cooker along with any collected juices. Add remaining ingredients and stir well.

✳ Position the pressure cooker lid and lock in place. Raise the heat to high and bring to high pressure. Adjust the heat to stabilize the pressure and cook for 15 minutes. Remove from heat and lower pressure using the cold-water release method (see note on page 59). Open the pressure cooker.

✳ Place the pressure cooker, uncovered, on a burner over high heat and reduce the sauce by half. Stir periodically so the chicken does not stick. Serve immediately.

SERVES 4

THIS RECIPE TYPIFIES THE best OF WHAT IT MEANS TO COOK IN A pressure COOKER. IT IS SIMPLE, ECONOMICAL, AND NUTRITIOUS. THE ADDITION OF beer AND YOGURT MAKES FOR A delicious SAUCE THAT ALSO TENDERIZES THE CHICKEN.

Braised Farmhouse Chicken

TOM LACALAMITA / REPRINTED FROM *THE ULTIMATE PRESSURE COOKER COOKBOOK*
(SIMON & SCHUSTER)

2 chicken breasts with bone, split (about
   2 pounds)
1/2 cup water
1/2 cup dry white wine
1/2 cup olive oil
1 bay leaf

8 cloves garlic, unpeeled
1 teaspoon paprika
2 teaspoons salt
1 tablespoon whole black peppercorns
4 threads saffron (optional)

✳ Remove and discard all the visible fat from the chicken. Cut the breast halves into 2 or 3 pieces, right through the bone. Place chicken in a pressure cooker. Add the remaining ingredients and stir to blend.

✳ Position the lid and lock in place. Place over high heat and bring to high pressure. Adjust the heat to stabilize the pressure and cook 15 minutes. Remove from heat and lower pressure using cold-water release method (see note on page 59). Open the pressure cooker.

✳ Place the pressure cooker, uncovered, on a burner over high heat and reduce the sauce by half. Stir periodically so that the chicken does not stick. Taste and adjust for salt.

✳ If serving with fried potatoes, place the potatoes on a large serving platter. Lay the chicken pieces on top of potatoes. Strain sauce to remove peppercorns and bay leaf and spoon the sauce over chicken and potatoes.

SERVES 4

AS THE CHICKEN BRAISES IN THE PRESSURE COOKER, THE cooking LIQUID COMBINES WITH THE NATURAL juices OF THE CHICKEN TO PRODUCE A FLAVORFUL, RICH SAUCE, WHICH IS TRADITIONALLY SERVED OVER MATCHSTICK-THIN potatoes FRIED WITH WHOLE, UNPEELED CLOVES OF GARLIC.

Monterey Stuffed Chicken Breasts

DENIS BLAIS, EXECUTIVE CHEF, PACIFIC PALISADES HOTEL, VANCOUVER, BRITISH COLUMBIA

SERVES 6

DENIS BLAIS, ONE OF VANCOUVER'S finest CHEFS, RECOMMENDS THIS RECIPE FOR home cooks WHO WANT TO MAKE SOMETHING ELEGANT AND EASY.

Filling
4 ounces leaf spinach
4 tablespoons butter
2 shallots, minced
1/4 pound sliced mushrooms
1/4 cup julienned sun-dried tomatoes
1 pound ricotta cheese
1/3 cup Parmesan cheese
1 teaspoon finely chopped dill
1 teaspoon finely chopped oregano
1 clove garlic, minced
Salt and freshly ground black pepper
    to taste
2 tablespoons bread crumbs

6 boneless, chicken breasts (inside fillet
    attached)
Salt and freshly ground black pepper

White Wine Dill Sauce
4 tablespoons butter
2 large shallots, minced
1 clove garlic, minced
1/4 cup white wine
1 1/2 cups brown veal stock
Juice of 1/2 lemon
1/3 cup heavy cream
1 tablespoon chopped fresh dill

✳ To prepare the filling, blanch the spinach in boiling, salted water for 10 to 15 seconds. Drain and cool under cold water. Squeeze out all excess moisture and chop coarsely.

✳ Warm butter in a small sauté pan. Add shallots and mushrooms and sauté over medium-high heat for 4 to 5 minutes, until soft. Drain in a sieve, reserving a couple tablespoons of the butter and set aside.

✳ Combine spinach, shallots, mushrooms, and the rest of the filling ingredients in a large mixing bowl. Mix thoroughly.

✳ Preheat oven to 350°F. Holding each chicken breast, pointed end down, firmly open cavity behind the inside fillet. Pack filling deep into cavity until plump. Use skin and fillet to tuck filling in.

✳ Place stuffed chicken breasts on a baking sheet. Brush with reserved butter and season with salt and pepper. Bake for 30 to 35 minutes, while making white wine dill sauce.

✳ To make white wine dill sauce, warm butter in a medium sauté pan. Add shallots and garlic and sauté over medium-high heat for 3 to 4 minutes, until soft. Add wine to deglaze pan, stirring with a wooden spoon to pick up any browned bits on the bottom of the pan. Add veal stock, bring to a boil, lower to a simmer, and reduce liquid by half.

✳ Add lemon juice and cream, bring to a simmer, and simmer to reduce until sauce is thick and shiny.

✳ Strain sauce through a fine-mesh sieve. Add dill and season with salt and pepper. Serve immediately over chicken breasts.

Narsai's Assyrian Chicken

NARSAI DAVID, FOOD AND WINE EDITOR, KCBS RADIO, SAN FRANCISCO, CALIFORNIA

2 whole boneless, skinless chicken breasts,
   split into halves
3 tablespoons vegetable oil
Salt
Flour
1 cup orange juice

1/2 cup white wine
Juice of one lemon
3 tablespoons honey
1/2 teaspoon ground ginger
Tabasco sauce or cayenne pepper, to taste
12 kumquats, thinly sliced

✳ Carefully pull away the "fillet" from each half breast (this is a small, elongated section attached to each breast half, sometimes referred to as a "supreme"). Cut the remaining breast meat into 3 or 4 strips the same size as the fillet.

✳ Heat the oil in a large skillet. While it is heating, salt the chicken pieces and flour them very lightly, shaking off any excess flour. (A good way to do this is to put the flour in a paper bag, add several pieces of chicken at a time, close the top, and shake well.) Sauté the chicken in the hot oil only until the pieces are heated through and have turned opaque. It is important to avoid overcooking them. Transfer the chicken pieces to a warm platter.

✳ Add the orange juice, wine, lemon juice, honey, ginger, and Tabasco sauce (or cayenne pepper) to the pan. Whisk to dissolve all the pan drippings and cook, uncovered, until liquid reduces to a thin sauce, about 5 minutes over high heat. Add the kumquats and return the chicken pieces to the pan. Stir just long enough to coat the chicken pieces with the sauce. Serve immediately.

SERVES 6

NARSAI DAVID, OF ASSYRIAN descent, USED HIS MOTHER'S COOKING AS AN inspiration FOR THIS FRUITY AND COLORFUL DISH.

Jerk Chicken

LORA BRODY / REPRINTED FROM *PLUGGED IN* (WILLIAM MORROW AND COMPANY)

1 chicken (about 3 1/2 pounds), skin
  removed and cut into 8 pieces
1 large onion, cut into 8 pieces
3 cloves garlic, peeled
1 generous tablespoon candied ginger
1 1/2 tablespoons canned chipotle chilies,
  or more to taste

1/2 teaspoon allspice
2 tablespoons mustard
1 teaspoon pepper
2 tablespoons balsamic vinegar
2 tablespoons soy sauce

✳ Place chicken in Crock-Pot.

✳ To prepare the sauce, place onion, garlic, and ginger in a food processor fitted with a metal blade. Process to pulverize. Add the rest of the sauce ingredients to the food processor and pulse to combine.

✳ Pour sauce over chicken in Crock-Pot and toss to coat.

✳ Cook chicken on a LOW setting for 6 to 8 hours, or on HIGH for 2 to 3 hours.

Grilled West Indies Spice-Rubbed Chicken Breast with Grilled Banana

CHRIS SCHLESINGER AND JOHN WILLOUGHBY / REPRINTED FROM *LICENSE TO GRILL* (WILLIAM MORROW AND COMPANY)

Spice Rub
3 tablespoons curry powder
3 tablespoons ground cumin
2 tablespoons allspice
3 tablespoons paprika
2 tablespoons powdered ginger
1 tablespoon cayenne pepper
2 tablespoons salt
2 tablespoons freshly ground black pepper

4 boneless chicken breasts, skin on
4 firm bananas, skin on and halved
    lengthwise
2 tablespoons vegetable oil
1 tablespoon soft butter
2 tablespoons molasses

Lime halves for garnish

✳ Mix all the spices together well, rub this mixture over both sides of each chicken breast, cover, and refrigerate for 2 hours.

✳ Start fire.

✳ Over a medium fire, grill the chicken breasts, skin side down, for 7 to 8 minutes, until well browned and heavily crusted. Turn them and grill an additional 10 minutes. Check for doneness by nicking the largest breast at the fattest point: the meat should be fully opaque with no traces of red. Remove chicken from the grill.

✳ Rub the banana halves with the vegetable oil and place them on the grill, flat side down. Grill them for about 2 minutes, or until the flat sides are slightly golden color. Flip them and grill for an additional 2 minutes.

✳ Remove the banana halves from the grill. Mix the butter and molasses together and paint this over the bananas. Serve the chicken breasts and banana halves together, sprinkled with a little lime juice.

SERVES 4

THE NORMAL searing AND CRUSTING ACTION OF GRILLING IS ENHANCED BY THE spice RUB, AND THE RESULT IS A SUPERCRUSTED, FLAVOR-CONCENTRATED SURFACE covering A MOIST BREAST.

Grilled Quail

CHRIS JOHNSON, EXECUTIVE CHEF, RAINCITY GRILL, VANCOUVER, BRITISH COLUMBIA

SERVES 6

A warming DISH FOR

A COOL EVENING.

6 whole quail
Salt and freshly ground pepper
6 jumbo or 18 medium shrimp, peeled
   and deveined
2 teaspoons turmeric
2 teaspoons dry mustard
1 tablespoon vegetable oil

16 baby carrots, trimmed and peeled
   (other seasonal vegetables of your
   choice can be substituted)
1 cup whipping cream
$1/2$ cup dark veal stock (available at
   specialty shops)
3 cups cooked wild rice

✳ Season quail with salt and pepper, inside and out. Season shrimp with salt and pepper. Mix together turmeric, dry mustard, and oil into a paste and rub into shrimp. Cover and refrigerate both quail and shrimp for 1 hour.

✳ Start a fire or turn gas grill to medium.

✳ Bring water to boil in a pot with a steamer rack. Add carrots, cover, and steam until carrots are tender. Remove carrots from pot and keep warm while cooking quail and shrimp.

✳ When coals are covered with gray ash and there is a gentle red glow underneath, place quail on grill. Cook for 4 minutes and turn. At this point, place shrimp on grill. After 2 minutes, turn shrimp. After 2 more minutes, remove both quail and shrimp.

✳ While quail and shrimp are cooking on grill, place cream and veal stock in a medium saucepan and simmer, whisking ingredients together. Simmer until reduced by about one-third, about 4 minutes, until thickened and sauce-like. Keep warm.

✳ Place ½ cup of cooked wild rice on a large soup plate. Place 1 quail and 1 large shrimp (or 3 medium shrimp) on each bed of rice. Arrange 4 carrots artfully on each plate. Spoon sauce over the dish and serve immediately.

Cornish Hen Under a Brick

ROZANNE GOLD / REPRINTED FROM *RECIPES 1-2-3* **(VIKING PENGUIN)**

1¹/₂-pound Cornish hen
Salt and freshly ground black pepper
3 tablespoons Garlic Oil (*see below*),
    plus additional for drizzling, if desired

¹/₂ cup dry white wine
1 tablespoon chopped fresh rosemary

✷ With kitchen shears, cut the hen along the length of the backbone. With your fist, pound the bird flat so that it is butterflied. Season with salt and pepper.

✷ Heat the oil in a large nonstick skillet. Place the hen, skin side down, in the oil and place a brick wrapped in aluminum foil on top. Cook over medium heat, turning every 2 to 3 minutes, replacing brick each time, for 10 to 12 minutes, or until golden brown. Remove hen to a large warm plate and keep warm.

✷ Add the wine and rosemary to the pan and reduce over high heat, scraping up the browned bits in the pan. When the sauce has thickened, pour it over the hen. Serve immediately. Drizzle with additional garlic oil, if desired.

Garlic Oil

16 medium cloves garlic
2 cups olive oil

2 California bay leaves
¹/₂ teaspoon whole black peppercorns

✷ Peel the garlic and place with oil in a small, heavy pot. Heat gently for 5 minutes, or until bubbles form on top. Remove from heat and add bay leaves and peppercorns. Let steep and cool. The garlic oil will last 2 weeks in the refrigerator. *Makes 2 cups*

SERVES 1 OR 2

YOU REALLY NEED A BRICK FOR MAKING THIS DISH, BECAUSE THE authentic ITALIAN PREPARATION REQUIRES THAT THE HEN LIE COMPLETELY FLAT WHILE cooking. YOU WILL BE REWARDED FOR YOUR efforts WITH ULTRA-CRISP SKIN AND succulent MEAT.

Chicken Jambalaya

REPRINTED FROM *JOY OF COOKING* (SCRIBNER)

2 tablespoons butter or vegetable oil
1 chicken (about 2^1/$_2$ pounds), cut into
　serving pieces, fat and excess skin
　trimmed
Salt and freshly ground black pepper
1 green bell pepper, cored, seeded,
　and diced
^{1}/$_2$ cup diced celery
1 cup long-grain white rice

^{1}/$_2$ teaspoon ground red pepper flakes
3 cups boiling water
^{1}/$_4$ cup chopped fresh parsley
^{1}/$_4$ teaspoon dried thyme
^{3}/$_4$ teaspoon salt
^{1}/$_8$ teaspoon freshly ground black pepper
1 bay leaf
1 cup slivered cooked ham (about 1 ounce)
　or 1 chorizo sausage, thinly sliced

✳ Heat butter or oil in a large skillet over medium heat. Add the chicken pieces and cook, turning frequently, until browned on all sides, about 10 minutes. Remove to a plate and season with salt and pepper to taste.

✳ To the drippings in the skillet used to cook chicken, add the green pepper, celery, rice, and red pepper flakes. Cook over medium-low heat, stirring to coat all the ingredients with the butter or oil.

✳ Add the boiling water, parsley, thyme, salt, pepper, and bay leaf. Return the chicken to the skillet and add cooked ham or sausage. Cover the skillet and cook over medium-low heat until the water is absorbed and the chicken is cooked through, about 20 minutes. Remove cover and continue to cook until all excess moisture is evaporated, about 3 minutes. Serve hot.

SERVES 4

JAMBALAYA IS A popular dish THROUGHOUT THE AMERICAN SOUTH, BUT IT IS MOST OFTEN ASSOCIATED WITH THE cooking OF NEW ORLEANS.

Pan-Seared Salmon with Orange-Basil Pesto

SOREN C. FAKSTORP, CHEF DE CUISINE, C RESTAURANT, VANCOUVER, BRITISH COLUMBIA

Orange Basil Pesto Sauce
4 whole oranges, peeled
2 shallots, peeled and diced
1/2 cup tightly packed basil leaves
1/4 cup balsamic vinegar
1 cup extra-virgin olive oil

Tomato Salad
6 to 8 tomatoes, different colors of
   heirloom varieties, if available, sliced
Juice of 2 lemons
1/2 cup olive oil
Salt and freshly ground black pepper

Onion Rings
Vegetable oil for deep-frying
2 red onion rings, peeled and thinly sliced
Flour for dredging

Salmon
2 tablespoons vegetable oil (if using
   a nonstick pan, no oil is needed)
Four 5-ounce boneless salmon fillets
Salt and freshly ground black pepper

SERVES 4

THIS colorful RECIPE IS MEANT FOR THE GLORY days OF SUMMER, WHEN BASIL AND heirloom tomatoes ARE AT THEIR PEAK.

✳ To make orange-basil pesto, place oranges, shallots, and basil in a blender or bowl of a food processor. Blend or process until smooth. Add vinegar and blend until smooth again. With machine running, add olive oil in a thin stream to create a smooth emulsion. Pesto can be made up to a day in advance and refrigerated. (Bring pesto to room temperature before using.)

✳ Shortly before serving, arrange sliced tomatoes in overlapping concentric circles on a dinner plate. Drizzle with lemon juice and olive oil. Season with salt and pepper and set aside at room temperature.

✳ Pour 1 inch of vegetable oil into a deep, medium-size skillet. Heat oil until a drop of water slides along surface of oil. While oil is heating, dredge onion rings in flour. Fry onion rings in hot oil until golden and crispy, 1 to 2 minutes. Keep onion rings warm while cooking salmon.

✳ In a large sauté pan, add the 2 tablespoons of olive oil. Season salmon fillets with salt and pepper, place in warm oil, and pan-fry until golden brown, 2 to 3 minutes per side.

✳ Place salmon fillets on top of tomatoes on serving plates. Spoon pesto on fish and top with onion rings. Serve immediately.

Satay-Glazed Vegetable Skewers with Cilantro Parmesan Noodles

STEVEN WONG / REPRINTED FROM *NEW WORLD NOODLES* **(ROBERT ROSE)**

1 recipe Cilantro Parmesan Noodles (*see page 99*)

8 bamboo skewers, soaked in water for 4 hours

2 zucchini, cut into a total of 16 slices, each about 1 inch thick

2 red bell peppers, cut into a total of 16 large squares

16 large mushrooms

Basting Sauce

1 tablespoon satay sauce (Chinese barbecue sauce)

1 tablespoon honey

1 tablespoon hoisin sauce

1 tablespoon soy sauce

1 tablespoon balsamic vinegar

2 tablespoons olive oil

✱ Prepare cilantro parmesan noodles and keep warm.

✱ Preheat broiler or, if using a grill, start fire.

✱ Thread skewers in an attractive arrangement, using 2 pieces of each vegetable for each skewer.

✱ In a small bowl, combine ingredients for basting sauce and mix well.

✱ Brush vegetable skewers with olive oil and broil, or grill for 1 minute on each side. Baste each side with sauce and continue cooking for another 2 minutes on each side or until vegetables are just tender. Continue to baste during cooking to ensure that the vegetables are well coated.

✱ Divide cilantro parmesan noodles among 4 plates. Top with cooked vegetables and serve immediately.

Cilantro Parmesan Noodles

STEVEN WONG / REPRINTED FROM *NEW WORLD NOODLES* **(ROBERT ROSE)**

1 pound fresh Shanghai noodles or
   fresh fettuccine
2 tablespoons heavy cream

1/2 cup freshly grated Parmesan cheese
1/2 cup chopped cilantro
Salt and freshly ground black pepper

✳ In a large pot of boiling salted water, cook noodles until al dente, about 3 minutes (if cooking fettuccine, prepare according to package directions). Drain.

✳ Immediately return noodles to pot. Over low heat, add cream and Parmesan and mix. Add cilantro and toss thoroughly to combine. Season with salt and pepper to taste. Serve immediately.

SERVES 4

THIS QUICK AND easy NOODLE DISH IS A GOOD ONE TO HAVE IN YOUR repertoire. SERVE WITH GRILLED CHICKEN AND A GREEN SALAD, OR WITH SATAY-GLAZED VEGETABLE skewers.

DESSERTS

Chocolate Cappuccino Mousse

MICHEL ROUX / REPRINTED FROM *FINEST DESSERTS* **(RIZZOLI)**

9 ounces finest-quality bittersweet
  chocolate
6 egg whites
1/2 cup plus 2 tablespoons sugar

4 egg yolks
1/2 cup heavy cream
1 tablespoon instant coffee powder
1 tablespoon sweetened cocoa powder

✳ Chop chocolate into thin pieces and place in a stainless steel bowl. Stand in a *bain-marie* (or water bath) set over medium heat. Remove from the heat as soon as the chocolate has melted.

✳ While chocolate is melting, beat the egg whites until half-risen. While still beating, add the sugar, a little at a time, and beat to a stiff peak.

✳ Stir the yolks, then ¼ cup of the cream into the melted chocolate and immediately fold in the beaten egg whites delicately with a rubber spatula. As soon as the mixture becomes homogeneous, divide it among 4 shallow serving bowls or wide-mouthed, shallow cups. Place in the refrigerator and allow to firm.

✳ Just before serving, dissolve the instant coffee in a scant 2 tablespoons water. With a fork or whisk, whip the remaining cream into a light, runny foam, then add the coffee. Top each mousse with the foam, sprinkle with a little cocoa, and serve immediately.

SERVES 4

THIS IS ONE OF THE MOST popular DESSERTS ON THE CELEBRITY CRUISE LINE, FROM THEIR EXECUTIVE CHEF, MICHEL ROUX. IT'S not difficult TO MAKE AND CAN BE MADE A DAY IN advance.

Dairy-Free Chocolate-Almond Cake

CLAIRE CRISCUOLO / REPRINTED FROM *CLAIRE'S CORNER COPIA COOKBOOK* (VIKING PENGUIN)

2$\frac{1}{4}$ cups unbleached white flour
4 teaspoons baking powder
$\frac{1}{4}$ teaspoon salt
1$\frac{2}{3}$ cups sugar
1 cup unsweetened cocoa

$\frac{1}{2}$ cup (1 stick) soybean margarine,
   softened to room temperature
$\frac{2}{3}$ cup soft tofu, crumbled and drained
1$\frac{1}{4}$ cups soy milk
1 teaspoon pure almond extract
1 cup slivered almonds

✳ Preheat oven to 350°F. Measure the flour, baking powder, salt, sugar, and cocoa into a bowl.

✳ Measure the soy margarine, tofu, soy milk, and almond extract into a blender. Cover and blend on low speed for 5 seconds. Stop to scrape down sides using a rubber spatula. Cover again and blend on high speed for 1 minute, stopping once to scrape down the sides.

✳ Pour the blended ingredients over the dry ingredients all at once. Beat lightly with a wooden spoon for about 30 seconds to mix. Stir in almonds.

✳ Spray a 10-inch Bundt pan with nonstick cooking oil spray.

✳ Turn the batter into the prepared pan, using a rubber spatula to scrape the bowl. Spread the batter smooth.

✳ Bake for about 50 minutes, until a cake tester inserted into the center comes out clean. Remove the pan from the oven and let set for 2 minutes before turning onto a cake dish.

Heavenly Chocolate Roll

LORA BRODY / REPRINTED FROM *PLUGGED IN* (WILLIAM MORROW AND COMPANY)

SERVES 10 TO 16

BESTSELLING COOKBOOK

AUTHOR LORA BRODY'S

family HAS MADE THIS

THEIR FAVORITE DESSERT

FOR birthdays AND

SPECIAL OCCASIONS.

Cake
8 extra-large eggs, separated and at room
    temperature
1¼ cups granulated sugar
Scant ⅓ cup cocoa (not Dutch process),
    plus extra for garnish
Scant ⅓ cup all-purpose flour, sifted

Filling
2 pints premium ice cream, softened

Topping
Hot Fudge Sauce (see page 105)
Whipped cream

✳ Preheat oven to 350°F.

✳ In a stand mixer with a paddle blade, beat the egg yolks until frothy. Turn mixer to high, add ½ cup of the sugar, and beat until the mixture is very thick and light yellow in color.

✳ Shift speed on mixer to low and add cocoa and flour. Blend only until ingredients are incorporated (do not overbeat). In a separate bowl, beat the egg whites with the remaining sugar until stiff, but not dry, as for a soufflé. Carefully fold the egg whites into the cocoa mixture.

✳ Pour the cocoa mixture into a 10 x 15-inch jelly roll pan that has been greased, lined with parchment paper, and greased again. Spread the mixture evenly with a spatula.

✳ Bake for 15 to 17 minutes, or until the edges just begin to pull away from the sides of the pan. Set the pan on a rack and cover the top of the cake with a slightly damp kitchen towel and allow to cool at room temperature, at least 1 hour.

✳ Sift a layer of cocoa evenly over the top of the cake. Cover with 2 long overlapping strips of plastic wrap. Cover with another baking sheet and invert cake onto plastic wrap and baking sheet. Carefully peel off parchment paper.

✳ Spread the softened ice cream over the cake, leaving 1 inch of unfilled border around the edges. Using the plastic wrap underneath as a guide, roll the cake like a jelly roll and slide seam of roll onto a board or platter. (Rolling from the long side gives an elegant, slender roll that can be cut into 14 to 16 small slices. Rolling from the shorter side produces a shorter, fatter roll and bigger slices.) Wrap cake roll in the plastic wrap or aluminum foil. Freeze for several hours.

✳ To serve, cut slices, pour hot fudge sauce over the top, and finish with whipped cream.

Hot Fudge Sauce

LORA BRODY / REPRINTED FROM *PLUGGED IN* **(WILLIAM MORROW AND COMPANY)**

8 ounces bittersweet chocolate, coarsely chopped

4 ounces unsweetened chocolate, coarsely chopped

3 tablespoons sweet butter, cut into small pieces

1/2 cup firmly packed brown sugar

2 cups heavy cream

✱ Place the chocolate, butter, and brown sugar in the work bowl of a food processor fitted with a plastic blade.

✱ Heat the cream in a 2-quart saucepan set over medium heat. As soon as bubbles appear around the edge of the pan, lower the heat and allow the cream to come to a boil. If the cream threatens to overflow the pan, lower the heat and stir vigorously with a wire whisk. Allow the cream to simmer for 15 minutes, stirring occasionally.

✱ With the processor off, pour the hot cream through the feed tube. Replace the plunger and process until smooth, about 20 seconds. This can also be done with a hand blender; be sure to use a deep bowl to avoid spattering.

✱ Use immediately over Heavenly Chocolate Roll (see recipe page 104) or store in a covered container in the refrigerator or freezer.

THIS HOT FUDGE SAUCE CAN BE MADE UP TO 2 WEEKS ahead. REFRIGERATE IN A COVERED CONTAINER AND warm IN THE MICROWAVE, OR FREEZE FOR up TO 6 MONTHS.

Deep-Dish Pizza Cookie

MARCEL DESAULNIERS / REPRINTED FROM *DEATH BY CHOCOLATE COOKIES* (SIMON & SCHUSTER)

SERVES 12 TO 16

DON'T EXPECT ANYONE TO deliver THIS PIZZA TO YOUR HOUSE! A SURPRIS-INGLY irresistible COMBINATION OF SWEET AND TART flavors REWARDS YOUR EFFORTS.

White Chocolate Pizza Crust
3 cups all-purpose flour
1 teaspoon baking powder
1/2 teaspoon salt
4 ounces white chocolate, chopped into 1/4-inch pieces
4 tablespoons granulated sugar
2 large egg yolks
1 teaspoon pure vanilla extract
12 ounces chilled unsalted butter, cut into 1-ounce pieces

Pizza Topping
1 cup pecans
1 cup heavy cream
1/4 cup tightly packed light brown sugar
2 cups dried cranberries
4 ounces finely diced dried apricots
4 ounces semisweet chocolate, chopped into 1/4-inch pieces
2 ounces white chocolate, chopped into 1/4-inch pieces

✳ To make the white chocolate pizza crust, preheat oven to 375°F. In a sifter combine the flour, baking powder, and salt. Sift onto a large piece of wax paper and set aside.

✳ Heat 1 inch of water in the bottom of a double boiler over medium heat. With the heat on, place 4 ounces of the white chocolate in the top half of the double boiler. Use a rubber spatula to stir the chocolate until completely melted and smooth, about 4 minutes. Transfer to a small bowl.

✳ In a large bowl whisk together the granulated sugar, egg yolks, and vanilla extract until combined and the sugar has dissolved. Add the melted white chocolate and whisk to combine. Set aside.

✳ Place the sifted dry ingredients and butter in the bowl of a stand mixer fitted with a paddle. Mix on low for 2 minutes, until the butter is cut into the flour and the mixture develops a coarse, mealy texture. Add the white chocolate mixture to the flour and butter mixture and mix on low for 30 seconds until a loose dough is formed.

✳ Transfer the dough to a clean, dry work surface and knead gently to form a smooth dough. Place the dough in a 9 x 3-inch springform pan and use your fingers to press the dough into the bottom and then three-quarters of the way up the sides of the pan. Place the pan on the center rack of the preheated oven and bake for 14 minutes. Remove the pan from the oven and allow to stand at room temperature while preparing the toppings.

(continued on next page)

✱ To prepare the pizza cookie topping, toast the pecans on a baking sheet in the preheated oven for 5 minutes. Remove the pecans from the oven and cool to room temperature before chopping into ¼-inch pieces.

✱ Heat the heavy cream and light brown sugar in a large saucepan over medium heat. When hot, stir to dissolve the sugar. Bring to a boil, adjust the heat, and allow to simmer for 6 minutes until slightly thickened. Remove from heat and add the dried cranberries, apricots, and toasted pecans; stir with a rubber spatula to combine.

✱ Pour the topping onto the cooled crust, using a rubber spatula to spread topping evenly over crust. Sprinkle the chopped semisweet chocolate evenly over the entire surface of the topping.

✱ Place the pan on the center rack of the preheated oven and bake for 30 minutes until lightly browned around the edges. Remove the pizza from the oven and allow to cool to room temperature for 1 hour.

✱ While pizza is cooling, again heat 1 inch of water in the bottom half of a double boiler over medium heat. With the heat on, place 2 ounces of the white chocolate in the top half of the double boiler. Use a rubber spatula to stir the chocolate until completely melted and smooth, about 3 minutes. Using a teaspoon, drizzle thin lines of white chocolate over the entire surface of the pizza topping. Allow the chocolate to become firm at room temperature before cutting.

✱ Remove the pizza from the pan and place on a cutting board. Using a serrated knife, cut the pizza into 12 to 16 slices. Store the pizza cookies in a tightly sealed plastic container until ready to serve.

Hazelnut Tea Cake

ROZANNE GOLD / REPRINTED FROM *RECIPES 1-2-3* (VIKING PENGUIN)

2 cups hazelnuts with skins (about 8 ounces)

2 extra-large eggs

1/2 cup pure maple syrup, plus 1 to 2 tablespoons for glaze

Grated zest of 1 orange

Pinch of salt

✳ Preheat oven to 350°F. Toast the nuts in a nonstick skillet over medium heat until you just begin to smell a faint nutty aroma. Remove from pan and allow to cool.

✳ Put the eggs, syrup, and orange zest in the warmed bowl of a stand mixer. Add salt and beat at medium-high speed for 6 to 7 minutes, until the mixture has increased substantially in volume.

✳ Grind the nuts finely in a food processor until powdery and mix into egg mixture. Pour into a nonstick 8½-inch loaf pan lined with waxed paper on the bottom.

✳ Place in oven and bake for 35 to 40 minutes, or until a toothpick inserted in the cake comes out clean. Glaze with 1 or 2 tablespoons of maple syrup and spread with a pastry brush. Let cool.

SERVES 8 TO 10

IT'S HARD TO believe THAT SO FEW INGREDIENTS CAN MAKE SUCH A SATISFYING CAKE. Enjoy WITH A CUP OF COFFEE OR TEA.

Chocolate Peanut Butter Bengal Cookies

MARCEL DESAULNIERS / REPRINTED FROM *DEATH BY CHOCOLATE COOKIES* (SIMON & SCHUSTER)

MAKES 4 DOZEN

2¹/₂-INCH COOKIES

MAKES 4 DOZEN

2 1/2-INCH COOKIES

PILE ALL OF YOUR favorite MEMORIES INTO ONE BOWL AND YOU HAVE THE RECIPE FOR THIS cookie. NOTE THAT THE RECIPE NEEDS TO BE STARTED AT LEAST 4 HOURS IN ADVANCE OF WANTING TO SIT DOWN WITH A GLASS OF milk OR CUP OF COFFEE AND THE cookies.

Cookies

1 cup unsalted peanuts
6 ounces semisweet chocolate, chopped
   into 1/4-inch pieces
1 cup creamy peanut butter
3/4 cup granulated sugar
1/4 pound unsalted butter, cut into
   1-ounce pieces
1 large egg
2 teaspoons pure vanilla extract
1 1/4 cups all-purpose flour
1/8 teaspoon salt

Topping

1 1/4 cups creamy peanut butter
1/4 cup confectioners' sugar

Chocolate Drizzle

8 ounces semisweet chocolate, chopped
   into 1/4-inch pieces

✳ Preheat oven to 325°F. Toast the peanuts on a baking sheet in the preheated oven for 10 to 12 minutes, shaking occasionally, until golden brown. Cool the nuts to room temperature before finely chopping, either in a food processor fitted with a metal blade (about 20 seconds) or by hand with a cook's knife.

✳ Heat 1 inch of water in the bottom half of a double boiler over medium heat. With the heat on, place 6 ounces of semisweet chocolate in the top half of the double boiler. Use a rubber spatula to stir the chocolate until completely melted and smooth, about 4 to 6 minutes. Transfer the melted chocolate to a small bowl and set aside.

✳ Place 1 cup of the peanut butter, the granulated sugar, and the butter in the bowl of a stand mixer fitted with a paddle. Beat on medium for 2 minutes until soft. Use a rubber spatula to scrape down the sides of the bowl. Add the egg and vanilla extract and beat on high for 3 minutes until smooth. Scrape down the sides of the bowl. Add the melted chocolate and the chopped peanuts and mix on medium until incorporated, about 1 minute. Operate the mixer on low while gradually adding the flour and salt. Remove the bowl from the mixer and use a rubber spatula to finish mixing the ingredients until thoroughly combined. Transfer the dough onto a dry, clean cutting board.

✲ Divide the dough into 2 equal portions. With both palms, roll each portion of dough to form cylinders 12 inches long and 1½ inches in diameter. Individually wrap each cylinder in plastic wrap and place in the refrigerator for 3 to 4 hours, until the dough is very firm to the touch.

✲ Preheat oven to 325°F. Remove the dough from the refrigerator and unwrap. Cut each piece of dough into 24 individual ½-inch-thick slices. Divide the slices onto 4 nonstick baking sheets—or bake cookies in batches—so that there are 12 evenly spaced slices per sheet. Place the baking sheets on the top and center racks of the preheated oven and bake for 16 to 18 minutes, rotating the sheets from top to center (and vica versa) halfway through the baking time (at that time also turn each sheet 180 degrees). Remove the cookies from the oven and cool to room temperature on baking sheets, about 30 minutes.

✲ To prepare the topping, place the peanut butter and the confectioners' sugar in the bowl of a stand mixer fitted with a paddle. Mix on low for 30 seconds. Use a rubber spatula to scrape down the sides of the bowl, then beat on high for 1 minute. Remove the bowl from the mixer and use a rubber spatula to finish mixing the ingredients until completely smooth. Set aside.

✲ To make the chocolate drizzle, heat 1 inch of water in the bottom half of a double boiler over medium heat. With the heat on, place 8 ounces of semisweet chocolate in the top half of the double boiler. Use a rubber spatula to stir the chocolate until completely melted and smooth, about 4 to 6 minutes. Transfer the melted chocolate to a small bowl and set aside until needed.

✲ To arrange the cookies, place a heaping teaspoon of topping in the center of each cookie. Use a small spatula or butter knife to spread the topping evenly over the top of the cookie. Use a teaspoon to drizzle thin lines of the melted chocolate onto the top of each cookie. Keep the cookies at room temperature for 25 to 30 minutes to firm the chocolate. Store the cookies in a tightly sealed plastic container until ready to serve.

Road Trip Cookies

MARCEL DESAULNIERS / REPRINTED FROM *DEATH BY CHOCOLATE COOKIES* (SIMON & SCHUSTER)

MAKES EIGHTEEN

4-INCH COOKIES

THE king OF CHOCOLATE,
MARCEL DESAULNIERS,
MAKES THESE cookies
FOR HIS LONG CAR TRIPS
AND JUDGES THE DISTANCE
TRAVELED BY THE NUMBER
OF cookies CONSUMED.

2 1/2 cups all-purpose flour
1 teaspoon baking soda
1/2 teaspoon salt
6 ounces semisweet chocolate, chopped
   into 1/4-inch pieces
3/4 cup granulated sugar

3/4 cup tightly packed light brown sugar
1/4 pound unsalted butter at room
   temperature
2 large eggs
2 teaspoons pure vanilla extract
1 1/2 cups peanut M & M's

✻ Preheat oven to 350°F. In a sifter combine the flour, baking soda, and salt. Sift onto a large piece of waxed paper and set aside until needed.

✻ Heat 1 inch of water in the bottom of a double boiler over medium heat . With the heat on, place the semisweet chocolate in the top half of the double boiler. Use a rubber spatula to stir the chocolate until completely melted and smooth, about 4 to 5 minutes. Transfer to a small bowl and set aside.

✻ Place the granulated sugar, light brown sugar, and butter in a large bowl. Use a stiff rubber spatula (or wooden spoon) to cream the ingredients together until smooth. Add the eggs and vanilla extract and mix to incorporate. Add the melted chocolate and mix until combined. Add the dry sifted ingredients and thoroughly combine. Add the M & M's, mixing to incorporate.

✻ Using 3 heaping tablespoons of dough for each cookie, portion 6 cookies, evenly spaced, onto each of 3 nonstick baking sheets—or bake cookies in batches (this is a hefty cookie, so don't crowd). Place the baking sheets on the top and center racks of the preheated oven and bake for 14 minutes.

✻ Remove the cookies from the oven and cool to room temperature on the baking sheets, about 30 minutes. Store the cooled cookies in a tightly sealed plastic container until ready to serve.

Dee-lux Layered Choco-Oat Bars

T.K. WOODS / REPRINTED FROM THE GREAT AMERICAN CHOCOLATE CONTEST COOKBOOK (WILLIAM MORROW AND COMPANY)

Crust

1/3 cup unsalted butter or margarine, melted

1 1/2 cups graham cracker crumbs

Filling

12 ounces semisweet chocolate chips

1 cup butter or margarine, melted

2 cups firmly packed light brown sugar

1 tablespoon hot water

2 large eggs, lightly beaten

2 teaspoons vanilla extract

2 cups all-purpose flour

1/4 teaspoon baking soda

1 teaspoon baking powder

1 teaspoon salt

1 1/4 cups Quaker Quick Oats

1 cup chopped walnuts (see note below on toasting)

Chocolate Topping (optional)

6 ounces semisweet chocolate chips

MAKES 30 BARS

NINA SCHONDELMEIER FROM WEST HARTFORD, CONNECTICUT, TOOK FIRST prize IN THE CHOCOLATE BAR CATEGORY FOR THIS DELECTABLE treat.

✳ To make the crust, preheat the oven to 350°F. Put the 1/3 cup of melted butter in the bottom of a 9 x 11-inch baking pan. Sprinkle the graham cracker crumbs on top and pat down firmly, covering the bottom of the pan and going 1/2 inch up the sides. Bake in oven for 10 minutes.

✳ To make the filling layers, immediately sprinkle chocolate chips on top of the crumb crust after removing it from the oven. Let the chips melt, then spread the melted chocolate evenly over the entire crust.

✳ In a large bowl, mix the 1 cup of melted butter with the brown sugar and add water. Add the eggs and vanilla. Mix well.

✳ In a separate bowl, sift together the flour, baking soda, baking powder, and salt. Stir the flour mixture into the creamed butter mixture. Add the oatmeal and mix well. Stir the walnuts into the batter.

✳ Spread the batter in the pan over the melted chocolate chips and bake for 30 minutes, or until the sides pull away from the pan.

✳ If you choose to make the optional chocolate topping, immediately sprinkle the chocolate chips over the bar as soon as it comes out of the oven. Allow chips to melt. Spread the melted chocolate over the bar. Allow the bar to cool in the pan on a wire rack for at least 1 hour before cutting into squares.

NOTE: For extra nutty flavor, spread the nuts on a cookie sheet and toast them in a preheated 350°F oven for 10 to 15 minutes, shaking pan occasionally to prevent nuts from burning.

Big Chunk Fresh Apple Pie

SHIRLEY CORRIHER / REPRINTED FROM *COOKWISE* (WILLIAM MORROW AND COMPANY)

Filling

1 cup chopped dates
1/2 cup boiling water
1/2 teaspoon baking soda
1 1/2 cups plus 1/2 cup chopped walnuts,
    pecans, or almonds
3 tablespoons plus 6 tablespoons lightly
    salted butter
1/8 teaspoon plus 3/4 teaspoon salt
2 tablespoons cornstarch
1/3 cup plus 1/2 cup cool water

1 tablespoon pure vanilla extract
10 medium Golden Delicious apples
    (about 5 pounds), peeled, each cut into
    8 wedges and each wedge cut in half
1 cup sugar
1 cup light brown sugar, packed
1 teaspoon ground cinnamon
1/4 teaspoon freshly grated nutmeg
1/3 cup fine cake or bread crumbs

2 prebaked crusts (*see pages 116–117*)

✳ An hour or so before preparing the pie filling, soak the dates in a bowl with the boiling water and baking soda.

✳ Preheat oven to 350°F. Place walnuts (or other nuts) on a baking sheet and roast in oven for 10 to 12 minutes, shaking pan occasionally. Remove from oven, place in a bowl, and while they are hot, stir in the 3 tablespoons of butter and 1/8 teaspoon of salt.

✳ Stir the cornstarch into the 1/3 cup of cool water in a small bowl. In another small bowl, stir vanilla into the 1/2 cup of cool water. Set both bowls aside.

✳ In a large skillet (or 2 skillets, if necessary), sauté the apple chunks in the 6 tablespoons of butter for 2 minutes over medium heat, turning gently with a large spatula. Add the vanilla mixture and simmer for 1 minute. Add the sugar, brown sugar, the 3/4 teaspoon of salt, cinnamon, nutmeg, and drained dates. Bring to a simmer and stir in cornstarch mixture. Continue to simmer until the liquid in the skillet is thick and bubbly. Add 1 1/2 cups of the roasted walnut mixture. Toss gently until the apples and walnuts are well coated with the liquid.

✳ Sprinkle the remaining 1/2 cup of walnuts and the crumbs over the prebaked bottom crust. Spoon in the apple mixture with a slotted spoon. If any liquid left in the skillet is thick, pour it over the apples. If liquid is thin, boil to thicken to a syrup, then spoon over the apples. Cover with prebaked Dome Leaf Pattern (or store-bought) top crust (see page 117). Serve hot or at room temperature.

SERVES 8 TO 10

DEPENDING UPON YOUR mood AND THE TIME AVAILABLE, THIS pie CAN EITHER BE MADE WITH STORE-BOUGHT CRUSTS OR THE UNUSUAL CRUST DESCRIBED HERE.

FINELY GRATED PARMESAN cheese IS ADDED TO THE CRUST TO ADD rich CHEESE flavor AND CREATE A WELL-BROWNED AND smooth CRUST.

Flaky Store-Bought Crusts

Bottom Crust

1 ready-to-bake pie crust
1 egg, lightly beaten
3 tablespoons grated Parmesan cheese

Top Crust

1 package (enough for two 9-inch crusts)
    fold-out pie crusts

✳ For the bottom crust, bake a frozen, ready-to-bake crust according to package directions. When it is done, glaze the edge with the beaten egg and sprinkle Parmesan cheese over the bottom. Place back in oven and bake until cheese is melted and glaze is shiny, about 4 minutes.

✳ For the top crust, buy fold-out crusts from the dairy or frozen foods section of your supermarket. Roll, cut, decorate, and bake according to directions outlined in the homemade crust recipe below (see "To prepare Dome Leaf Pattern Top Crust" on page 117).

Flaky Homemade Crust

2 cups bleached all-purpose flour
1/2 cup instant flour (Wondra or Shake
    and Blend)
1/2 teaspoon salt
1 stick (4 ounces) butter, cut into
    1/2-inch cubes
6 tablespoons butter-flavored shortening,
    in tablespoon-size pieces

1/3 cup finely grated Parmesan cheese
1/4 teaspoon freshly grated nutmeg
1/8 teaspoon cayenne
One 8-ounce container of sour cream
Ice water
Nonstick cooking spray
1 large egg, beaten

✳ Place both flours, salt, and butter in a bowl in the freezer for 10 minutes. Place shortening on a small plate in the freezer for the same amount of time.

✳ Dump cold flour-butter mixture onto a clean work surface. Roll over mixture with a rolling pin to flatten butter lumps. Scrape butter off the pin and scrape mixture back into a pile. Roll over flour mixture again, scrape back together, and roll over dough a third time. Scrape back into the bowl and place back in the freezer for 10 minutes.

✳ Remove flour-butter mixture from freezer and dump onto a clean counter. Add cold shortening pieces and roll over mixture with a rolling pin, scrape together and roll over again. Scrape back into the cold bowl that was used in freezer and add Parmesan cheese, nutmeg, and cayenne and stir once. Add sour cream and stir until dough comes together. Add a tablespoon or two of ice water if necessary. Cover the dough and place in the refrigerator for 30 minutes.

✳ Remove the dough from the refrigerator. Divide dough in half and shape each piece into a 6- to 8-inch disc about ¾ inch thick. Cover each piece with plastic wrap. Place one disc back in the refrigerator to be used for the Dome Leaf Pattern Top Crust.

✳ Place other disc on a lightly floured work space. Roll disc out by rolling forward with rolling pin, then back, taking care not to roll off the dough. Rotate the dough a quarter turn, roll forward and back again. If dough is sticking to counter or pin, flour lightly.

✳ Cut a 12-inch circle from the dough, lightly flour the top, fold in half, then fold in half the other way so that you have a quarter circle.

✳ Spray a 9-inch pan with nonstick cooking spray. Place folded dough in the pan with the point in the center. Unfold the dough so that it covers the pan. Fold under about ½ inch of the crust all the way around, making a double-thick edge to flute. Flute edge, place in the refrigerator for 20 minutes and then move to the freezer.

✳ Preheat the oven to 400°F. After the crust has been in the freezer for 10 minutes, remove and cover with parchment paper or aluminum foil. Fill the covered crust with pennies, beans, rice, or pie weights to hold down crust.

✳ Bake crust for 15 minutes in the center of the oven. Remove weights and parchment (or foil). Push crust down firmly and bake again for 5 to 7 minutes, to dry crust out. Glaze with beaten egg and bake until glaze is shiny, about 3 minutes. Allow to cool before filling with apple mixture.

✳ **To prepare Dome Leaf Pattern Top Crust,** roll out the other dough disc (that has been in refrigerator) as for the bottom crust. With a pizza wheel or sharp knife, cut out a 12-inch circle. Turn a 9- to 10-inch round-bottom stainless steel bowl upside down and spray the bottom with nonstick cooking spray. Place the circle of dough on it.

✳ From the scraps, make branches by rolling strips of dough between the palm of your hand and the counter and then twisting them. Cut leaves and press vein patterns into each leaf. Stick the leaves and branches onto the dough by dampening them with a few drops of water and pressing. Twist or curl up the edges of the leaves so that they stand up and have a three-dimensional effect. Have some of the stuck-on branches curl over themselves and cross on top of or under leaves. Carefully place the bowl and decorated dough in the freezer for 15 minutes.

✳ Place the upside-down bowl on a shelf in the lower third of the oven and bake for 15 to 20 minutes until deep brown. Cool before placing on top of filled bottom crust.

Italian Celebration Cake

TOM LACALAMITA / REPRINTED FROM *ESPRESSO DESSERTS* (SIMON & SCHUSTER)

Espresso Pastry Cream

2¹/₂ cups milk
¹/₂ cup espresso coffee beans, coarsely
    chopped
4 large eggs
4 large egg yolks
1 cup granulated sugar
4 tablespoons unbleached
    all-purpose flour

Sponge Cake

1 cup unbleached all-purpose flour
1 teaspoon baking powder
4 large eggs, separated, plus 1 whole
    large egg
²/₃ cup granulated sugar
Pinch of salt

2 tablespoons dark rum mixed with
    ¹/₄ cup water (optional)
1 package (3 ounces) soft ladyfingers
¹/₃ cup sliced almonds

SERVES 8

ITALIANS, WHO ARE GENERALLY NOT BIG ON DESSERTS, WOULD MAKE THIS FOR A special OCCASION. THE LADY-FINGERS THAT CIRCLE THE cake CREATE A BEAUTIFUL FINISH.

✳ To prepare the pastry cream, bring milk and coffee beans to a boil in a medium-size saucepan. Remove from heat, cover, and let sit 10 minutes. Pour into a second saucepan through a fine-mesh strainer. Discard the coffee beans.

✳ In a large mixing bowl, beat together the whole eggs, yolks, sugar, and flour until well combined. Bring the coffee-flavored milk to a boil. Lower the heat and gradually whisk in the egg mixture. Stir constantly until the pastry cream begins to thicken and comes to a boil. Remove from heat and pour the cream into a nonreactive bowl. Cover with a piece of plastic wrap, pushing the plastic into the custard so that a skin does not form. Let cool.

✳ To prepare the sponge cake, preheat the oven to 375°F. Butter and flour a 9-inch round cake pan. Sift the flour and baking powder into a large mixing bowl. Set aside.

✳ Beat the egg yolks, whole egg, and ⅓ cup of the sugar in a large mixing bowl until the mixture is thick and lemon-colored. Fold in the flour mixture. Set the batter aside.

✳ In a large bowl, beat the egg whites with salt until stiff peaks form. Gradually add the remaining ⅓ cup sugar and beat until glossy. Fold one-third of the batter into the beaten egg whites, until incorporated. Repeat process two more times. Pour the batter into the prepared pan and bake until the cake is golden and springs back when pressed, 20 to 25 minutes. Let cool 10 minutes, then remove the cake to a wire rack to cool completely.

✳ To assemble the dessert, cut cake in half horizontally once it has cooled. Place one half, cut side up, on a large serving plate. Sprinkle, if desired, with half of the diluted rum, then spread with one-third of the pastry cream. Place the second layer of cake, cut side down, on top of the first. Sprinkle, if desired, with the remaining diluted rum, then spread with half of the remaining pastry cream. Gently break the ladyfingers in half, lengthwise. Attach them around the perimeter of the cake, broken side down, by spreading them with the remaining pastry cream. Cover the top of the cake with sliced almonds.

Frontera Grill's Chocolate Pecan Pie

RICK BAYLESS / REPRINTED FROM *RICK BAYLESS'S MEXICAN KITCHEN* (SCRIBNER)

SERVES 12

RICK BAYLESS PUT THIS

RECIPE together

THINKING THAT BY

STIRRING CHUNKS OF

CHOCOLATE INTO A PECAN

pie FILLING HE COULD

MAKE THIS favorite

FROM BOTH SIDES OF

THE BORDER SEEM LESS

cloying. HE WAS RIGHT,

ALTHOUGH THE RESULT IS

STILL WONDERFULLY RICH.

Crust

1^1/$_2$ cups all-purpose flour

6 tablespoons chilled unsalted butter, cut into ^{1}/$_2$-inch bits

3 tablespoons vegetable shortening, cut into ^{1}/$_2$-inch bits

^{3}/$_4$ teaspoon sugar

^{1}/$_4$ teaspoon salt

Ice water

1 egg yolk, beaten slightly

Filling

2 cups pecan halves (make sure they're fresh and flavorful)

6 ounces semisweet or bittersweet chocolate

3 tablespoons all-purpose flour

^{3}/$_4$ cup (1^1/$_2$ sticks) room-temperature unsalted butter

1 cup firmly packed dark brown sugar

5 large eggs, at room temperature

^{3}/$_4$ cup light corn syrup

^{1}/$_4$ cup molasses

1^1/$_2$ tablespoons Kahlúa or brandy

2^1/$_4$ teaspoons pure vanilla extract

^{1}/$_2$ teaspoon salt

2 cups Sweetened Whip Cream (*see page 121*) for serving

✳ To make the dough, measure the flour, butter, and shortening into a bowl or a food processor fitted with a metal blade. Quickly work the fats into the flour with a pastry blender or pulse the food processor until the flour looks a little damp (not powdery), but tiny bits of fat are visible. If using a food processor, transfer the mixture to a bowl.

✳ Mix together the sugar, salt, and 3 tablespoons of ice water in a small bowl. Using a fork, little by little work the ice-water mixture into the flour mixture. The dough will be in rough, rather stiff clumps; if there is unincorporated flour in the bottom of the bowl, sprinkle in a little more ice water and use the fork to work it together. Press the dough together into a flat disk, wrap in plastic, and refrigerate at least 1 hour.

✳ On a lightly floured surface, roll the dough into a 12-inch circle. Transfer to a deep 10-inch glass pie pan (Rick Bayless suggests rolling the dough onto the rolling pin, then unrolling it onto the pie pan). Decoratively crimp the edge and trim excess dough. Refrigerate 30 minutes.

✳ To prebake the crust, preheat the oven to 400°F. Lightly oil a 15-inch piece of foil and lay it, oiled side down, into the crust (heavy-duty aluminum foil is too stiff to work here);

press down to line the crust snugly. Fill with beans or pie weights and bake about 15 minutes, until beginning to brown around the edges. Reduce the oven temperature to 350°F. Carefully remove the beans (or weights) and foil, return the crust to the oven, and bake 8 to 10 minutes, until it no longer looks moist. (If crust bubbles at this point, gently press it down with the back of a spoon.) Brush the beaten egg yolk over the crust, then let cool completely.

✷ While the crust is cooling, spread the pecans on a baking sheet and toast in a 350°F oven until fragrant, about 10 minutes. Cool, then break into small pieces and transfer to a large bowl. Chop the chocolate into rough, ½-inch pieces and add to bowl, along with the flour. Stir until everything is well coated.

✷ To make the filling, cream the butter and brown sugar in a food processor (or in a large bowl of a stand mixer) until light and fluffy, about 3 minutes in the food processor, 5 minutes in the mixer. With the machine still running, add the eggs 1 at a time, letting each be completely incorporated before adding the next. Beat in the corn syrup, molasses, Kahlúa or brandy, vanilla, and salt.

✷ To bake the pie, pour the filling over the chocolate and pecans and stir well to combine. Pour the mixture into the prebaked pie shell, set onto the lower rack of the oven and bake until a knife inserted into the center is withdrawn clean, about 1 hour.

✷ Cool pie completely on a wire rack. Serve slices of the pie at room temperature or slightly warm, topped with a dollop of Kahlúa-spiked, Sweetened Whip Cream.

Sweetened Whip Cream

1 cup heavy cream
1 tablespoon powdered sugar

1 teaspoon vanilla extract
1 tablespoon Kahlúa

✷ With either a stand mixer or by hand, whip cream until it holds a luscious, soft peak, then whip in sugar, vanilla extract, and Kahlúa. *Makes 2 cups*

Swiss Chocolate Truffle Cake

NICK MALGIERI / REPRINTED FROM *HOW TO BAKE* (HARPERCOLLINS)

1 recipe Viennese "Saddle of Venison"
Cake batter, without the cinnamon
(*see page 124*)

Filling

24 ounces (1½ pounds) semisweet
chocolate

2 cups heavy cream

3 tablespoons unsalted butter

3 tablespoons light corn syrup

Unsweetened cocoa powder for
finishing cake

✴ Set rack in the middle of the oven and preheat to 350°F.

✴ Spread the cake batter on an 11 x 17-inch jelly roll pan buttered and then lined with a sheet of parchment or waxed paper. Bake for 20 minutes or until firm. Slide the cake from the pan to cool on a rack.

✴ To make the filling, cut up the chocolate into fine pieces and set aside. Combine the remaining ingredients in a medium saucepan and bring to a boil. Remove from the heat, add the chocolate, and allow to stand for 5 minutes. Whisk chocolate mixture until smooth and strain through a medium-mesh sieve into a bowl. Refrigerate until thickened. Immediately before using the filling, whisk gently.

✴ To assemble the cakes, cut the baked layer into 6 pieces, each about 4 x 8 inches. Place 2 of the pieces on 4 x 8½-inch cutouts of cardboard to make handling easier. Spread each piece with a thin layer of filling. Cover each piece with another layer of cake and spread filling on those. Place the last layer on each cake and mask the sides of each cake with a thin layer of filling.

✴ Divide the remaining filling in half and place half on the top of each cake. Smooth the filling into a wedge shape on top of each cake; slant the short ends upward toward the center of the cake. Chill the cakes to set the filling, and very lightly dust with cocoa powder before serving. The cakes may be wrapped and frozen for a month after filling has set.

SERVES 16

AN ADAPTATION OF THE truffle CAKE FROM THE FAMOUS SPRUNGLI PASTRY SHOP IN ZURICH. THIS DESSERT IS easy TO MAKE IN ADVANCE AND AS IT makes TWO CAKES, ONE MAY BE USED IMMEDIATELY AND THE OTHER REFRIGERATED OR frozen FOR LATER USE.

Viennese "Saddle of Venison" Cake

NICK MALGIERI / REPRINTED FROM *HOW TO BAKE* (HARPERCOLLINS)

SERVES 12 TO 15

IN VIENNA, THIS RICH chocolate CAKE IS BAKED IN A RIDGED, SEMI-CYLINDRICAL PAN. AFTER THE CHOCOLATE icing IS POURED OVER THE UNMOLDED cake, IT IS STUCK WITH PIECES OF SLIVERED ALMOND, RESEMBLING A TIED, LARDED, AND SAUCED roast. HENCE THE NAME, "SADDLE OF VENISON" CAKE.

Cake
6 ounces semisweet chocolate
12 tablespoons (1 1/2 sticks) unsalted butter
2/3 cup sugar
8 large eggs, separated
1 1/3 cups (about 5 ounces) blanched or
  unblanched ground almonds
2/3 cup dry bread crumbs
1 teaspoon ground cinnamon

Glaze
1 cup currant jelly

Icing
1/3 cup water
1 cup sugar
1/3 cup light corn syrup
8 ounces semisweet chocolate

1 cup slivered almonds
Whipped cream for serving

✳ Set a rack in the middle of the oven and preheat oven to 350°F. Butter and flour a 10-inch round cake pan.

✳ To make the cake batter, cut the chocolate into fine pieces and place in a small bowl over hot water to melt (or use a double boiler), stirring occasionally. Set aside to cool.

✳ Beat the butter with 1/3 cup of the sugar until the mixture is soft and light. Beat in the chocolate, then the egg yolks, 1 at a time.

✳ In a small bowl, stir together the almonds, crumbs, and cinnamon, then stir into mixture.

✳ In a clean, dry bowl with clean, dry beaters, beat the egg whites until they hold a soft peak, then beat in the remaining 1/3 cup of sugar in a slow stream. Continue to beat the egg whites until they hold a firm peak.

✳ Stir a quarter of the egg whites into the batter, then fold in the rest with a rubber spatula. Pour the batter into the prepared pan and bake for 40 minutes, until the cake is well risen and firm. Unmold the cake onto a rack to cool.

✳ For the glaze, bring the currant jelly to a boil over medium heat. Lower the heat and simmer until the jelly is sticky and slightly thickened. Paint this glaze over the cooled cake.

✳ To make the chocolate icing, combine the water, sugar, and corn syrup in a saucepan and bring to a boil over low heat, stirring to dissolve the sugar completely. While it is cooking, cut the chocolate into fine pieces. Remove from the heat, add the chocolate, and allow icing to stand for a minute. Whisk until smooth.

✳ Position the cake on a rack with a jelly roll pan underneath. Pour the icing over the cake. Repair any uncovered areas with the icing that has dripped into the pan. Remove the cake to a platter before the icing has a chance to harden. Insert the pieces of slivered almonds in rows, at an angle, all the length of the cake. Serve the cake with whipped cream.

Chocolate Decadence

NARSAI DAVID, FOOD AND WINE EDITOR, KCBS RADIO, SAN FRANCISCO, CALIFORNIA

1 pound semisweet chocolate
1¼ sticks sweet butter
4 eggs
1 tablespoon sugar
1 tablespoon flour

Whipped Cream Frosting
1½ cups cream
1 teaspoon vanilla
1 tablespoon sugar

Raspberry Purée
One 10- to 12-ounce package frozen
  raspberries

✳ Preheat oven to 425°F.

✳ Melt chocolate with butter in a double boiler until just melted. Pour into a bowl and set aside. Wash top of double boiler, place over water in bottom of double boiler and bring water back to a boil.

✳ Place eggs and sugar in top of double boiler and beat until sugar dissolves and mixture is lukewarm (do not overcook). Remove from heat and whip until about quadrupled in volume.

✳ Fold flour into eggs. Then stir one-fourth of egg mixture into chocolate and butter. Then fold entire chocolate and sugar mixture back into remaining egg mixture.

✳ Pour batter into an 8-inch cake pan that has been buttered, floured, and the bottom lined with parchment paper. Bake in preheated oven for 15 minutes, and no longer. (Cake will be liquid in the center.) Remove pan from oven, allow to cool, and freeze, preferably overnight, before removing from pan.

✳ Before removing dessert from freezer, make whipped cream and raspberry purée. Whip cream with vanilla and sugar until soft peaks develop. Defrost raspberries, purée in blender, and press through a fine sieve to remove seeds.

✳ To remove chocolate decadence from pan, carefully dip bottom of pan in hot water to unmold dessert. Top with whipped cream, masking any faults. Refrigerate until ready to serve.

✳ To serve, slice dessert into 12 pieces. Either drizzle 2 to 3 tablespoons of raspberry purée onto plate followed by a slice of chocolate decadence, or drizzle raspberry purée over a slice of chocolate decadence on the plate.

SERVES 12

CHOCOLATE DECADENCE was developed AT NARSAI'S, AN award-winning RESTAURANT IN THE SAN FRANCISCO AREA FROM 1970 UNTIL 1986.

NOTES

INDEX

PERMISSIONS

From *Smoothies* by Mary Corpening Barber, Sara Corpening, and Lori Lyn Narlock (Chronicle Books, 1997) © 1997 by Mary Corpening Barber, Sara Corpening, and Lori Lyn Narlock: Banana Latte Smoothie, Classico Smoothie, Dangerously Red Smoothie, Dew It! Smoothie

From *Good n' Healthy!* by Brenda C. Ward and Jane Cabiness Jarrel (Tommy Nelson, a division of Nelson-Word Publishing Group, 1995) © 1995 by Brenda C. Ward and Jane Cabiness Jarrel: Breakfast Pizza

From Williams-Sonoma Outdoor Series: *Cabin Cooking* by Tori Ritchie (Time-Life, 1998) © 1998 Weldon Owen, Inc.: Brown Sugar Bacon, Cabin Potatoes, Puffed Oven Pancake, Summer Squash Frittata

From *Cookwise* by Shirley Corriher (William Morrow and Company, Inc., 1997) © 1997 by Shirley O. Corriher: Touch of Grace Biscuits, Big Chunk Fresh Apple Pie

From *How to Bake* by Nick Malgieri (Harper-Collins, 1995) © 1995 by Nick Malgieri: Neapolitan Ricotta, Mozzarella, and Prosciutto Pie; Swiss Chocolate Truffle Cake; Viennese "Saddle of Venison" Cake

From *Joy of Cooking* by Irma S. Rombauer, Marion Rombauer Becker, and Ethan Becker (Scribner, 1997) © 1997 by Simon and Schuster, The Joy of Cooking Trust, and the MRB Revocable Trust: New Orleans Bread Pudding with Southern Whiskey Sauce, Seviche, Chicken Jambalaya

From *The Best of Thai and Vietnamese Cooking* (Prima Publishing, 1997) © 1997 by Mai Pham: Sizzling Saigon Crèpes, Vietnamese Dipping Sauce, Rice Paper-Wrapped Salad Rolls, Hoisin-Peanut Sauce

From *Party Food* by Barbara Kafka (William Morrow and Company, Inc., 1992) © 1992 by Barbara Kafka: Beef Empanadas

From *Fresh from the Farmers' Market* by Janet Fletcher (Chronicle Books, 1997) © 1997 by Janet Fletcher: Bruschetta with Sweet Peppers and Ricotta, Spaghettini with Red and Gold Cherry Tomatoes, Green Bean Salad with Cherry Tomatoes and Ricotta Salada

From *Rick Bayless's Mexican Kitchen* by Rick Bayless (Scribner, 1996) © 1996 by Richard Lane Bayless: Rustic-Style Soup with Tomato, Jalapeño, and Avocado; Grilled Steak with Spicy Guajillo Sauce; Frontera Grill's Chocolate Pecan Pie

From *Claire's Corner Copia Cookbook* by Claire Criscuolo (Viking, 1997) © 1997 by Claire Criscuolo: French Peasant Soup, Dairy-Free Chocolate Almond Cake

From *The Greek Vegetarian* by Diane Kochilas (St. Martin's Press, 1996) © 1996 by Diane Kochilas: Villager's Leek and Fennel Pie, Christoforo Veneris's Eggplant Stuffed with Onions and Kefalotiri

From *James McNair's Burgers* by James McNair (Chronicle Books, 1992) © 1992 by James McNair: Knecht Burgers, New California Patty Melts, Three Nut Turkey Burgers

From *Recipes 1-2-3* by Rozanne Gold (Viking, 1996) © 1996 by Rozanne Gold: Orecchiette with Endive and Sun-Dried Tomatoes, Black Olive Tapenade, Cornish Hen Under a Brick, Hazelnut Tea Cake

From *Roasting* by Barbara Kafka (William Morrow and Company, Inc., 1995) © 1995 by Barbara Kafka: Roasted Red Pepper Spread, Soothing Summer Turkey Salad

From *James McNair's Grains and Beans* by James McNair (Chronicle Books, 1997) © 1997 by James McNair: Roasted Garlic and Bean Spread with Crusty Bread

From *Claire's Classic Vegetarian Cooking* by Claire Criscuolo (Dutton, 1997) © 1997 by Claire Criscuolo: Tuscan Salad of Chicory, White Beans, and Hearts of Palm

From *Salad Days* by Marcel Desaulniers (Simon & Schuster, 1998) © 1998 by Marcel Desaulniers: Roasted Root Vegetable Slaw with Gingered Apples, Raisins, Walnuts, and Barley

From *New World Noodles* by Steven Wong (Robert Rose, Inc., 1997) © 1997 by Steven Wong and Bill Jones: Shredded Chicken Salad with Spicy Sesame Vinaigrette, Peppered Beef with Flat Rice Noodles, Satay-Glazed Vegetables with Cilantro Parmesan Noodles

From *License to Grill* by Chris Schlesinger and John Willoughby (William Morrow and Company, Inc., 1997) © 1997 by Christopher Schlesinger and John Willoughby: Latin-Flavored Coleslaw with Grilled Avocados, Eggplant and Tomato Hobo Pack with Lemon and Garlic, Orange–Sweet Potato Pack, Grilled West Indies Spice-Rubbed Chicken Breast with Grilled Banana

From *The Foods and Flavors of Haute Provence* by Georgeanne Brennan (Chronicle Books, 1997) © 1997 by Georgeanne Brennan: Cabbage Salad with Prosciutto, Beef Daube with Dried Cèpes

From *The Ultimate Pressure Cooker Cookbook* by Tom Lacalamita (Simon & Schuster, 1997) © 1997 by Thomas N. Lacalamita: Home-Style Stuffed Artichokes, Chicken with Yogurt and Beer, Braised Farmhouse Chicken

From *James McNair Cooks Italian* by James McNair (Chronicle Books, 1994) © 1994 by James McNair: Baked Dumplings, Roman Style, Chicken Cutlets with Prosciutto and Sage

From *Potager* by Georgeanne Brennan (Chronicle Books, 1992) © 1992 by Georgeanne Brennan: Savory Bread Pudding Layered with Asparagus, Fontina, and Mixed Herbs

From *Sauces* by Michel Roux (Rizzoli, 1996) © 1996 by Michel Roux: Yogurt Sauce, Bois Boudran Sauce

From *The Great American Meatloaf Contest Cookbook* by Peter Kaufman and T.K. Woods (William Morrow and Company, Inc., 1994) © 1994 by Sparkatects, Inc.: Chicken Cordon Bleu Meatloaf, Popeye Meatloaf

From *Finest Desserts* by Michel Roux (Rizzoli, 1995) © 1994 by Michel Roux: Chocolate Cappuccino Mousse

From *Death by Chocolate Cookies* by Marcel Desaulniers (Simon & Schuster, 1997), © 1997 by Marcel Desaulniers: Deep-Dish Pizza Cookies, Chocolate Peanut Butter Bengal Cookies, Road Trip Cookies

From *The Great American Chocolate Contest Cookbook* by T.K. Woods (William Morrow and Company, Inc., 1995) © 1995 by Sparkatects, Inc.: Dee-Luxe Layered Choco-Oat Bars

From *Espresso Desserts* by Tom Lacalamita (Simon & Schuster, 1995) © 1995 by Thomas N. Lacalamita: Italian Celebration Cake

The following recipes are courtesy of

Narsai David:
Australian Flax and Sesame Seed Bread, Narsai's Assyrian Chicken, Chocolate Decadence

Denis Blais:
Smoked Salmon Napoleons, Monterey Stuffed Chicken Breasts

Chris Johnson:
Grilled Ratatouille, Grilled Caesar Salad, Grilled Quail

Soren C. Fakstorp:
Pan-Seared Salmon with Orange-Basil Pesto

Home Cooking with Amy Coleman © 1998 by Marjorie Poore Productions
Photography by Darla Furlani

Design and project management: Kari Perin, Perin+Perin
Editing: Cate Conniff Dobrich
Production: Kristen Wurz
Proofer: Sharilyn Hovind
Index: Ken DellaPenta

ISBN 0-9651095-2-6
Printed by Penn&Ink/Colorcraft, Hong Kong

10 9 8 7 6 5 4 3 2 1

MPP Books
363 14th Avenue, San Francisco, CA 94118

The **KitchenAid**® Story

A HUMBLE BEGINNING *The modern KitchenAid stand mixer began with a single drop of sweat off the end of a busy baker's nose. The year was 1908, and Herbert Johnston, an engineer and later president of the Hobart Manufacturing Company in Troy, Ohio, was watching the baker mix bread dough with an age-old iron spoon. To help ease that burden, Johnston pioneered the development of an eighty-quart mixer. By 1915 professional bakers had an easier, more thorough, and more sanitary way of mixing their wares.*

In fact, that amazing, labor-saving machine caught on so quickly that the United States Navy ordered Hobart mixers for its three new battleships—The California, The Tennessee, and The South Carolina. By 1917 the mixer was classified as "regular equipment" on all U.S. Navy ships.

The success of the commercial mixer gave Hobart engineers inspiration to create a mixer suitable for the home. But World War I interfered, and the concept of a home mixer was put on hold.

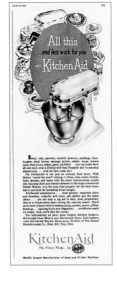

1919

THE BIRTH OF A KITCHEN ICON

1919 was truly a time of change. The gray days of war were giving way to the gaiety of the Roaring Twenties. The spark of women's suffrage had ignited and women across America would soon earn the right to vote. America was on the brink of an era of peace and prosperity, and progress was the cry from the factory to the farm.

War munitions plants across the country were busily converting to peace-time production. Meanwhile, a small manufacturing company in a sleepy, southwest Ohio town revived its effort to design the first electrical "food preparer" for the home.

And so it did! The first home stand mixer was born in 1919 at the Troy Metal Products Company, a subsidiary of the Hobart Manufacturing Company. The progeny of the large commercial food mixers, the Model H-5 was the first in a long line of quality home food preparers that utilized "planetary action." Planetary action was a revolutionary design that rotated the beater in one direction while moving it around the bowl in the opposite direction.

The wives of Troy executives tested the initial prototypes. While discussing possible names for the new machine, one homemaker commented, "I don't care what you call it, but I know it's the best kitchen aid I have ever had!" Hence, a brand name was born, and the first KitchenAid stand mixer was unveiled to the American consumer.

> ## "I don't care what you call it, but I know it's the best kitchen aid I have ever had!"

The KitchenAid H-5 rolled off the newly founded KitchenAid Manufacturing Company's assembly line at the rate of four per day and was priced at $189.50. The overriding concern then, as now, was that every KitchenAid produced would be of unsurpassed quality. Nothing would be shipped to customers that was not tested and retested.

But retail dealers were reluctant to undertake the selling of the unique "food preparer." So KitchenAid set out to sell its stand mixers door-to-door with a largely female sales force (strong enough to carry the 65-lb. Model H-5 on sales calls). Homemakers were encouraged to invite friends to their homes, where the KitchenAid salesperson would prepare food for the group showcasing the new stand mixer. By the 1930s the KitchenAid had earned wide acceptance, and dealers began to show interest.

1920–1930s

MEETING THE CONSUMERS' NEEDS

In the mid-1920s production had increased to five mixers per day, which was considered excellent efficiency by the standards of the day. Prices had declined to $150 (approximately $1,500 in today's dollars), and the company offered an easy payment program of 10% down and 10% per month for 10 months with no interest.

By the late 1920s American kitchens were growing smaller. KitchenAid responded with a smaller, lighter stand mixer at a lower price. The Model G proved so popular that the Model H-5 was stopped.

1930s

The 1930s brought the Depression, and with it, rising unemployment. The model G was beyond the financial means of most Americans, so KitchenAid confronted the problem. Within three years Kitchen-Aid introduced three new models that were less expensive and within the means of many American households.

In the midst of the great dust bowl years, social upheaval, and joblessness, KitchenAid planners laid a solid foundation that would support the stand mixer's growth for the next six decades. KitchenAid recruited Egmont Arens, a nationally acclaimed editor and world-renowned designer, to design three new stand mixer models. Arens's designs were so timelessly simple and functional that they remain virtually unchanged to this day.

1937

THE MODEL K

The Model K, first introduced in 1937, was more compact, moderately priced ($55), and capable of powering all the attachments. Every model introduced since has allowed for fully interchangeable attachments—a tribute to common sense and management of resources.

By the late 1930s, demand for KitchenAid stand mixers was so great that the factory could not keep up and sold out before Christmas each year. But in 1941 World War II intervened and the plant focused its production on munitions. During the war years there was limited production of KitchenAid stand mixers.

> ...the name KitchenAid has become synonymous with quality to generations of Americans.

As peace arrived and the troops came home, production of the KitchenAid stand mixer began again in earnest. KitchenAid moved to Greenville, Ohio, to expand the production. Greenville, is still the home of the factory where the dedicated employees of that community have proudly produced the stand mixer, and now other KitchenAid products, for more than half a century.

1950–1997
SEEN IN ALL THE BEST PLACES

KitchenAid, always in the forefront of trends, introduced daring new colors at the 1955 Atlantic City Housewares Show. The new colors—Petal Pink, Sunny Yellow, Island Green, Satin Chrome, and Antique Copper—were a bold departure from the white appliances seen in most kitchens of the time. To this day KitchenAid offers the standard classics, along with a variety of decorative colors.

Today, the legacy of quality lives on not only in the multifunctional stand mixer, but also in a full line of kitchen appliances sold across the world. Every product that carries the KitchenAid name, whether purchased in Paris or Peoria, is guaranteed to be strong, reliable and versatile—each backed by over 75 years of quality and excellence.

The distinctive silhouette of KitchenAid appliances can be seen in some of America's most famous home and restaurant kitchens. "Home Cooking" with Amy Coleman—which KitchenAid is proud to sponsor as part of an ongoing commitment to nurturing the talents of home chefs—marks the latest of many cooking shows that have relied on KitchenAid appliances to perform faultlessly and enhance the decor of their sets. Viewers of "Friends," "Cybill," and other television shows will see the appliances prominently displayed, and even used on occasion, in these sitcom kitchens. And finding a top restaurant without at least one hard-working KitchenAid stand mixer would be a real challenge.

Even museums, the ultimate showcases for design excellence, feature KitchenAid products on display. San Francisco's avant-garde Museum of Modern Art, for example, featured the KitchenAid stand mixer in an exhibit of American icons. There is even a KitchenAid stand mixer in the esteemed collection of the Smithsonian Institution.

From humble beginnings among the cornfields of southwest Ohio, the name KitchenAid has become synonymous with quality. Although over the years KitchenAid has streamlined and updated its stand mixer design and technology, the worldwide success of KitchenAid can be traced to the solid foundation set back in 1919.